UNDERSTANDING DREAMS

D0976390

UNDERSTANDING DREAMS

How to benefit from the power of your dreams

by

Nerys Dee

Thorsons
An Imprint of HarperCollinsPublishers

Thorsons
An Imprint of HarperCollins*Publishers*
77–85 Fulham Palace Road,
Hammersmith, London W6 8JB
1160 Battery Street
San Francisco, California 94111–1213

First published by Aquarian 1991
Thorsons edition 1995
5 7 9 10 8 6 4

© 1991 Nerys Dee

Nerys Dee asserts the moral right
to be identified as the author of this work

A catalogue record for this book
is available from the British Library

ISBN 1 85538 086 2

Typeset by G&M, Raunds, Northamptonshire
Printed in Great Britain by
HarperCollinsManufacturing Glasgow

All rights reserved. No part of this publication may be
reproduced, stored in a retrieval system, or transmitted,
in any form or by any means, electronic, mechanical,
photocopying, recording or otherwise, without the prior
permission of the publishers.

CONTENTS

INTRODUCTION

When we understand our dreams, we begin to understand ourselves. Since we, and we alone, create our dreams for individual, personal reasons, the best, indeed the only, person to unravel the messages they convey is oneself. Throughout the ages there have been many approaches to dreams — mythological, religious, scientific and analytical. These all offer explanations which tend to encourage us to look outside ourselves for meanings and answers, instead of inside, where we single-handedly create our own dreams.

These outer-approaches to dreams and their meanings are invaluable for comparing our dreams with those of others and for discovering traditional and social significances relating to certain objects and symbols we find in them. Dream dictionaries are the ultimate expression of external dream interpretation, but many of the signs and symbols we use are unique and have personal meanings only. These vary, depending on individual experiences, beliefs, inherited cultural traditions and present-day society. An example of this is the sun as a symbol. In western tradition it is a sign of life, energy and renewed hope. Metaphorically, those upon whom 'the sun shines' are said to be fortunate in the extreme. If, on the other hand, you live or originate from hotter climates, this same sun may well be seen as a menace and a threat to existence.

Similarly, if, as a child, you were badly sun-burned in any land, traditional meanings would soon be over-shadowed by personal memories of pain and suffering.

We need, therefore, to complement outer interpretation with inner understanding, thus making a blend of intellect and intuition, head and heart. All problems can be looked at in two distinctly different ways — practically or emotionally. Usually, when we are awake and thinking consciously, we view problems and situations from the practical, literal point of view, but when we are asleep and dreaming, these same problems and situations are seen from an intuitive and symbolic standpoint. This is looking at life from the inside, not from the outside. When we can do this, we are able to blend the two together, thus receiving the best of both worlds.

In dreams, inspirations are born, original ideas develop, acceptance is learned and solutions are found. How often have we gone to sleep tormented by a worry, to find on waking, that things are not quite as bad as they were yesterday? This is because we have 'slept on it' and allowed our hearts, which remain mostly silent during the day in the presence of our intellect, to speak to us throughout the night.

Understanding what we are saying to ourselves in a dream is very important; once we know they are potential sources of wisdom offering guidance in ways totally different from those found in the waking, outer world, there is no reason why we cannot usefully accept their bounty, as others have done in the past. For example, many inventors have discovered their unique creations through dreaming, just as some composers have first heard their own masterpieces in their sleep. Authors, too, have observed scenes and plots in a dream-state which, when set to words, have proved best-sellers.

The ancients knew all about this inner source and its keeper, and made conscious efforts to contact it. To help themselves in facing life's problems, they used to 'incubate a dream'. This simply means requesting the right dream at the right time. To do this they would retire to special temples and request help from the priestesses, priests, goddesses, gods, and sometimes from God Himself. Now, because most people regard their dreams as the incoherent ramblings of a worried mind, they rarely experience important dreams, and when they do, it is more by luck than judgement. Once we accept that dreams are inner sources of help, however, they, or that aspect of ourselves which produces them, respond immediately. Today there are no such temples but this does not mean that the age of creative dreaming belongs to the past. Far from it. Now, we can become our own priest or priestess and call upon our own forces, in our own inner temple.

CHAPTER ONE

THE DREAM DIARY

We dream every night but are not always able to remember them. Even so, the events encountered during sleep leave an unconscious message which colours our feelings towards daytime activities and problems. However, unless we are really interested in our nocturnal experiences, the chances are that they will fade from our memory soon after waking. If, on the other hand, we accept that they can sort out fact from fiction and offer us solutions to problems that we cannot solve during the day, then our dreams will respond with ever increasing enthusiasm.

To work with our dreams, which really means working with a lesser-known aspect of ourselves, we do need to remember them, and the best way to do this is to keep a Dream Diary. The fact that we intend to do this seems to remind our unconscious in some way, and even those who believe they 'never dream' find that, on waking, they soon remember at least one dream. There are no rules related to keeping a Dream Diary, but it helps if you follow a few practical, simple guidelines.

The best book you will ever read about dreams is the one you write yourself. It is, of course, none other than your own Dream Diary, so begin this today.

The Diary

The Commitment

Make a special effort to purchase a suitable notebook and pen specifically for the purpose of recording your dreams. This practical commitment is the first step towards understanding your inner self; it is also ritualistic in alerting your unconscious to the fact that you acknowledge that which it has to offer.

Once you have your diary and pen, place them by your bedside and make sure that they remain in the same place. Should they not be there on waking, you may well have lost a most valuable dream by the time you have found them.

The Number, Time and Date

It is important that you number each dream. You will then be able to see how many you have each night and how many over a period of time. You will find this varies considerably, a variation which you may be able to associate with the time of year, personal problems, positivity, negativity or other personal factors.

If the exact time you have a dream is known (this coincides with waking time) write it down as well. This encourages serial dreaming. For example, should you awake at 2am and write down a dream, you can then, with a little practice, return to that dream, should you wish to.

The date of each dream is most important, too. On looking back, you will find many were prophetic yet, at the time of the dream, such foresight was not recognised. Dating also reveals sequences and serial dreams as well as anniversaries which show the dreaming mind to be a fantastic calendar and cosmic clock in addition to its many other amazing characteristics.

Speed

Since dreams fade quickly from memory it is essential that they are captured as soon as possible. This means writing them down immediately on waking. Any delay means loss of valuable material. Reaching for your pen on opening your eyes soon becomes a habit and within a few days you will have conditioned yourself to do this. So, on waking, write down as quickly as possible as much as you can. You can always fill in details afterwards, so if it is a particularly long dream, write down the theme first of all. If you cannot remember anything whatsoever of your night's events, write down instead your mood. This will give you a clue concerning its theme and message. In fact, the waking mood sets the trend for the day. If it is happy, then the day will at least begin on a positive note. If, on the other hand, the initial mood is gloomy, we feel we have 'got out of the wrong side of the bed', as the saying goes, and things may well go wrong from the start.

Recording Your Dreams

Atmosphere, Mood and Feeling

The most important aspect of a dream is its atmosphere or mood, in other words 'the feel of a dream'. This not only colours our day but, when the dream is remembered, it gives a clue concerning its message. A residual haunting, gloomy, romantic or frightening feeling, for example, sets the scene before which the rest of the dream action takes place, so try to think of this as a backcloth for your dream stage.

Themes

The theme of a dream reveals the object and subject under observation, so look for this next. It may be a journey, a quest or seeking, waiting for someone or something, or it may be about a fear or hope for the future. There are literal themes as well as metaphorical and symbolic themes, so look for these too. Discovering this tells you the reason for the dream — it also helps to give it a title.

Characters, Objects, Signs and Symbols

Next, note the characters seen in your dream. Some will be known to you but others will not. Unknown characters may be acting as stand-ins, that is they represent someone else, or symbolise certain principles in life. A policeman, for example, stands for authority, law and order, just as your mother in your dream may not be drawing attention to herself, but instead represents motherliness and other feminine qualities within you.

'Characters' include creatures and monsters. Again, some of these you will recognise, such as pigs, cows, cats and dogs. Others could be mere shapeless things which chase you. When investigating the message behind these, their metaphorical meanings are important. For example, we often refer to others as pigs, cows, cats and dogs-in-the-manger, and the menacing shape is often no more than our own shadow-self who is urging us not to run away from an obvious truth.

When looking for objects in your dreams note any cars, trains, houses, cups, trees, etc. Each of these will have a special meaning in the language of dreams. Among these you may find unrecognisable objects ranging from strange mechanical devices to unusual food, representing latent inventiveness and desires for a fuller, more exotic life.

Signs and symbols will, on occasions, also be found in your dreams. Signs act as signposts indicating which direction you should take in life, whereas symbols offer glimpses of both the inner, personal world and the collective, outer dimension. In these lie apparent answers to the mysteries of life.

Movement and Travel

Few dreams depict still-life scenes. Most have action in one form or another. Travelling, for example, denotes your way through life — your destinational path. The way you do this in a dream reveals a great deal about the effort you are putting into your life, whether you are 'taking a ride' at the expense of someone else, or in control of your own driving force. Walking and running tells you self-generated effort will help you to achieve your aim, whereas travelling on a crowded bus or train warns that you are being carried along with the rest of humanity and it is time to 'get off the bandwagon' and stand more on your own feet.

Bus stops and railway stations are resting places but one does not want to stay there too long. Such a discovery is a sign pointing out that you must make up your mind where you are going in life. Missing a train or bus is a common occurrence in a dream too, clearly warning you not to miss an opportunity when it turns up.

Colours and Conversations

Most dreams are in colour but, like a dream itself, this fades leaving only the impression in black and white. If colour does not play a significant part, that is, if it does not have a specific message to impart, it is not registered. Dreams, among other things, are economical. Sometimes the colour of a dream is linked with its atmosphere, mood or feeling. An over-all grey scene relates to a grey or dull situation. Sunshine, on the other hand, offers a message of hope on the horizon. Individual colours in your dream should be noted because the seven colours of the rainbow — red, orange, yellow, green, blue, indigo and violet — each have a special dream-meaning, similar to that of waking awareness.

RED relates to physical energy: in its positive form it offers an improvement in health; in its negative form it suggests antagonism — the proverbial red rag to a bull.
ORANGE is a friendly colour associated with social activity and cheerfulness. Depending on the circumstances this colour is either telling you to cheer up, or pointing out that you need to.
YELLOW is the colour of sunshine and relates to intellectual matters. It is a clear colour, so seeing this in your dream tells you to think with your head — your intellect — to solve a problem.
GREEN means peace and relaxation. You either need more of this or you can expect it in the future, if this colour predominates.
BLUE is the colour for protection. This ties in with the blue sky which protects the earth from harmful radiation. Seeing blue in a

dream may, therefore, indicate that you need to protect yourself in some way or, conversely, you are feeling 'blue'.

INDIGO symbolises intuitive and instinctive qualities so this colour encourages you to allow your heart, the seat of inner feeling, to rule for a while.

VIOLET, the colour nearest to heaven, symbolises spiritual aspirations and religious beliefs.

Conversations in your dream can themselves be colourfully symbolic and may include puns, sentences which at first appear to be nonsense, rhymes, keywords, numbers and apparently meaningless letters. Many words have double meanings so conversations may be in code, but since it is the dreamer who concocts them, the clue to their solution is also somewhere, within the dreamer.

Previous Associations

Events from the previous day often reappear in dreams as an action replay. A television programme from the night before may be used by your dreaming mind to convey a personal situation, or some past experience might be conjured up to draw attention to a particular problem, hope or aim that needs special understanding, so look for the link between past happenings and the present dream. These will reflect certain likenesses providing valuable information which, when piecing together all the component parts noted in your Dream Diary, goes to make up the dream as a whole.

Having recorded all the different aspects relating to a dream you will have transformed the scene and action into words, which serves as a permanent reminder. Later in the day, if not immediately convenient, write out your dream in detail. Do not, however, delay for too long, as time will tend to rob you of valuable details and evidence.

A Page From Your Diary

Dream 1
Day and Date: Wednesday, 6th June 1990
Time: Between 6.00am and 7.30am
Number: 37
Feeling/Atmosphere: Perplexing
Theme: Lost in unknown territory
Movement/Travel: Driving car
Objects, Signs etc: Car, roads, trees, map
Colours/Conversations: Dark — no colours, no conversation
Previous Association: None recalled

The Dream — 'Lost'

I was driving a car, not mine, down twisting lanes, and did not
seem to know where it was leading. It was getting dark and no one
was around to ask if I was on the right road. The map was open but
I did not look at it. On waking I felt quite frightened. This feeling
stayed with me most of the day. It was difficult to relate to a
personal fear.

Remembering Dreams

Some dreams are so real they make strong impressions which make
them hard to forget. Others, however, are fleeting while yet others
vanish without a trace. One way to remember them is positively to
programme yourself before going to sleep. By appealing to the
power of your creative imagination you can link a dream with your
memory. This aspect of your unconscious is always ready to receive
suggestions so all you have to do is to visualise and talk to yourself
in a determined way.

   Once you feel ready to go to sleep, turn your attention to
dreams. Think of previous ones if you can. Then, relax by

breathing in to the count of three, and breathing out to the count of ten. Repeat this twice more, then breathe normally. Without moving, imagine you have just woken up in the morning and as you do, you reach for the pen and write down a dream. Bring your attention back to the present and become aware of feeling comfortable and warm. Finally, before dropping off to sleep, speak to yourself, saying 'In the morning I shall remember my dreams.'

The best book you will ever read on dreams is the one you write yourself. This is, of course, your Dream Diary.

CHAPTER TWO

DREAMS AND SLEEP

Every night we go to sleep and, to all intents and purposes, we are 'dead to the world'. We have to sleep in order to dream and each night, when we slip off into that unconscious state which would be frightening in the extreme if we were not so familiar with it, we visit another world — the world of dreams.

Although we now know a little about the condition scientifically, physiologically and psychologically, its real purpose is not fully understood. Until the twentieth century the only access we had to sleep came from remembered dreams but, with the advent of electronic monitoring of brain activity, certain information and discoveries have been made.

The Purpose of Sleep

For centuries the purpose of going to sleep was thought to be solely to rest the physical body. Having worked hard during the day, it needed to relax, so we went to sleep. This reasoning fell into disrepute when it was realised that resting while awake rejuvenated muscles in much the same way as in sleep. Furthermore, the body did not lie still during sleep; a series of time-lapsed photographs revealed that the body makes frequent movements — turning over as often as twenty times in a night, and stretching continually — in order to *exercise* the muscles, not to relax them.

Having realised this, it was decided it was not physical rest we needed during sleep after all, but psychological rest. The brain, the most important and active organ in the body, had, so it was thought, to be 'switched off' during sleep. This assumption again proved wrong. When it was possible to measure electronic impulses from the brain, it was found to be more active during sleep than when awake. Experiments involving sleep deprivation revealed unexpected results. By waking sleeping subjects throughout two consecutive nights it was discovered that, through lack of sleep, they were mentally disturbed and disorientated. Some years ago a US disc jockey named Peter Tripp decided to stay awake for 200 hours to raise money for charity. At the beginning of this sleepathon he was in good spirits and broadcast daily from Time Square. Later, his speech became slurred and towards the end of this stint it was incoherent. He then became paranoic, believing someone was drugging his food to make him go to sleep. He completed his 200-hour sleepless marathon and the only treatment he needed to restore his balance was a good, long sleep.

From this, and other experiments, it was discovered that lack of sleep harms both the body and the mind. If, then, sleep rests neither the body nor the mind, what, indeed, is it for? The advent of space travel gave scientists further opportunities to investigate this thing called sleep. They proved once again that resting the body is not the specific function of sleep. They also found that prolonged periods of isolation decreased the need for sleep. In other words, the less interaction there is between people, and the less stimuli received from external contact, the less sleep is needed.

Older people who have difficulty in sleeping may well be suffering from nothing more than lack of contact with others and deprivation of external stimuli. Apparently, we have a sleep control centre in the brain stem, at the base of the brain, associated with activity during wakefulness. When it is overloaded, it produces feelings of fatigue and eventually sleep. Lack of stimuli from the outer world, while causing drowsiness and disinterest in life, is not always sufficient to trigger this mechanism into sleep. Hence the problem of insomnia in institutionalised geriatrics and the reason why 95% of them are given sleeping tablets. Boredom and lack of stimuli may also account for insomnia in younger people. The paradox, however, is that over-stimulation causing anxiety also produces insomnia.

Brain Waves and the Dreaming Mind

Falling asleep follows lying down and relaxing the body, then the mind. Once asleep, the heart and breathing rate slows down, blood pressure is lowered and the body temperature drops slightly. The exact moment of going off to sleep is impossible to determine, even with the help of an electroencephalogram. The difference between being awake and being asleep is loss of conscious awareness. An external noise, for example asking a question, does not evoke a response.

Dream laboratories may not discover the reason for sleep or even what it is but, nonetheless, investigations have revealed some very interesting discoveries. Using computer language some researchers, comparing the brain with a computer, say we are 'off-line' during sleep. This means that the brain, like some computers, is not idle or resting but is reassessing, filing and up-dating the day's input. This would certainly seem to be the case, but it is taking the analogy too far when it is said that the brain, like the computer, jettisons all out-of-date data in the form of meaningless dreams. Since dreams are memories, no memory can be totally eradicated, so the jettison theory is too mechanical and simplistic. According to this reasoning our dreams are mere siftings worth nothing more than the rubbish bin. Such a notion, in the light of inventive, creative, prophetic and lucid dreaming, is nonsense.

To understand sleep we need to understand the brain. It was found earlier this century that the brain gives off electrical impulses and by the 1920s scientists could measure two different types of waves which they called Alpha and Beta. Later, as electrical devices improved, Delta, Theta, Mu, Gamma, Vertex, Spike and K waves have been found as well. To obtain these readings, electrodes are attached to various areas on the head and impulses are intensified and transformed into wave motions on graphs or into electroencephalograms on computer screens — EECs for short.

Interpreting what these waves mean is far from clear, and individual researchers each had their own names for them: 'deep and light phases'; 'active and quiet phases'; 'desynchronised and synchronised phases'; 'high and low phases', and finally 'paradoxical and orthodox phases' were terms used to describe dreaming and non-dreaming brain waves.

REM and Non-REM Sleep

In the 1960s it was clear that brain waves altered from Beta to Alpha when a subject closed his or her eyes. This was thought to be due to cutting off visual impulses from the outer world. It was further discovered that sleep, a stage beyond closing the eyes, could be divided into six levels which were labelled A, B, C, D, E and F. A represented light sleep and B, C, D, E and F levels represented progressively deeper sleep.

Associated with these levels are two distinct types of sleep. These have been called REM (Rapid Eye Movement) and NREM (non-REM) sleep. Early sleep, known as 'quiet sleep', is NREM sleep. There are several NREM phases throughout the night, the first lasting approximately 90 minutes, followed by a short REM phase which lasts about 10 minutes. Throughout the night NREM and REM phases alternate. Initially, the NREM stages are longer, then, as the night progresses, they become shorter and the REM phases take up the majority of sleeping time.

REM sleep is recognised by small twitches of facial muscles and slight movements of the hands. If snoring occurs during NREM sleep, this stops and breathing becomes laboured. Arms and legs are paralysed and the sleeper is unable to move. Blood pressure rises and the heartbeat increases as if the body is under physical exertion. Most significant of all, the eyes begin to move rapidly from side to side under closed eyelids, as if looking at a moving object. Researchers have discovered that when a sleeper within the REM stage is awakened, they invariably say they had been dreaming.

It is in the level of sleep recognised as F, that is, deep REM sleep, that eye movement is greatest. It is known that visual dreaming takes place during these phases but what was not realised until recently was that when those in NREM phases were awakened, they too thought they were dreaming. Subjects who were constantly awoken during the night (in particular during REM sleep which meant they were deprived of visual dreaming), became irritable, nervous, bad tempered and behaved out of character generally. It can, therefore, be concluded that *we sleep so that we can dream.*

How Much Sleep Do We Need?

We spend approximately one-third of our lives asleep. This means that when we reach the age of seventy-five, we have been asleep for twenty-five years. Babies sleep for over fifty per cent of their first year and, since most of this is in REM sleep, it is presumed they are dreaming visually. In fact they sleep and dream even before they are born. Adolescents sleep for eleven to twelve hours a night, adults seven to eight and older people seldom sleep for more than six hours during the night. This suggests we need slightly less sleep as we grow older.

Towards the end of the day we grow increasingly tired, both physically and mentally. Our bodies are heavy, we cannot concentrate, our eyes close involuntarily and we know that the only cure for this is to go to sleep. We, as human beings, are not alone in experiencing this all-consuming lethargy. Virtually every living organism is similarly affected. All mammals and birds sleep, so do fish and reptiles, albeit briefly. Even plants follow the diurnal and nocturnal cycles with their flowers closing their petals even before the sun goes down, and opening them again in the morning just before it rises. These cycles, the circadian rhythms, are daily fluctuations which seem to affect not only creatures and plants, down to their living cells, but the whole of nature as well.

Examples of this phenomenon on a grand scale are the rising and setting of the sun, the tides and the four seasons which, in turn, affect the breeding, seeding and dying of all species. Circadian rhythms also control sleep. We sleep when an internal clock in our brains gives the signal to our bodies telling it to stop daytime activity and slumber for a precise length of time.

Our internal clock, in common with the birds and plants, 'switches us off' at night. If we alter this pattern — an example is travelling from London to New York — we experience jet-lag. This condition is caused by breaking our circadian rhythm and even if we sleep for eight hours, beginning six hours later than usual, we cannot immediately adapt to the different rhythm. Our internal time-clock keeps telling our body it is six hours earlier. A change of sleeping pattern, therefore, does not mean we have lost sleep but rather that our inner-clock is out of phase with local time.

The Source Revisited

It has been concluded that, since resting the body and mind do not depend on sleep, its specific purpose must be to allow us to dream. During sleep our awareness reaches out to undiscovered realms, the land of dreams or, as C.G. Jung called it, the collective unconscious. This could well be the source from whence we came before we were born, and the place to which we return when we die. Do babies, therefore, who dream for most of their early life, revisit this source, our spiritual home?

Not all dreams, of course, are profound journeys to the great beyond. Many are literal action replays of real-life events, but even these take on a different significance when viewed from this inner standpoint. When, at night, we do return to the source, we enter a dimension far more expansive than the limited outer world. Here, we recharge with vitality following a physically active day, and when we are ill sleep is often the only healing force we need to recover.

To combat the stress and strain of life, relaxation and meditation are often resorted to, but these practices do not mitigate or remove such stress and strain. These are the result of circumstances with which we cannot cope and daytime techniques such as these are an apology for insufficient sleep. Few adults have enough of this and wonder why they always feel tired and cannot cope with problems. It is impossible to recharge when awake, for only in sleep can we contact the source and receive that essential vitality.

Some people can manage with less than seven hours sleep each night but they are, along with those who need over nine or ten, in the minority. The person who is occupied physically and mentally throughout the day needs an average of eight hours sleep. The test to know if you are having sufficient sleep is quite simple. If the alarm clock has to awaken you, it means you have not completed a REM or NREM cycle, so you are depriving yourself of valuable sleep. And if this happens five mornings out of seven, this deprivation is considerable and would account for loss of concentration, irritability, depression and many other unreasonable reactions to outer-world encounters and problems.

'Sleep', as Shakespeare so wisely put it, 'is the balm for hurt minds, nature's great second course'.

CHAPTER THREE

DREAMS AND THINGS THAT GO BUMP IN THE NIGHT

During sleep we have dreams, but we also have other experiences which are not, in the true sense of the word, dreams. Physiological and psychological changes take place during sleep, so experiences we may call 'dreams' are, in fact, the manifestation of these changes in dream form. When the sleep pattern changes from NREM to REM, considerable physiological changes take place. The heart begins to pound heavily and there is a rise in blood pressure; muscle tone is also affected.

These sensations are transformed into scenes which either incorporate or symbolise the feeling. Sounds are also used in this way by our dreaming mind. An example of this is the dreamer who dreamed she was in a room with her husband listening to an aeroplane overhead. The aeroplane stopped and she said to her husband 'I hope it is not going to crash'. Suddenly, the engine restarted. She awoke and realised that the aeroplane engine that stopped and started in her dream was none other than the intermittent snoring of her husband.

Smells are also integrated into dreams. When a dreamer moved into a flat over an Indian restaurant, he began to have dreams about nutmegs (the only spice he knew); this shows how the dreaming mind tries to logicize as well as symbolize.

Health and Dreams

Traditionally, it was thought that every disease produced a characteristic dream as a warning sign. Chest complaints were said to manifest as fights. When we speak of 'fighting for breath', we are, perhaps, glimpsing the origin of this belief. Many illnesses do, in fact, express themselves in dream form but not consistently enough to be totally reliable as warning signs. For example, a high fever is often interpreted by the dreaming mind as a fire. Similarly, a pain which is not sufficient to wake us but is nevertheless disturbing, may be symbolised as a thorn in the flesh, the pounding of sledgehammer or a wild animal biting into our body in the region of the pain.

Kidney complaints and problems associated with the urinary tract were, not surprisingly, said to conjure up scenes of water and over-full rivers, while seeing a canal in a dream heralded a birth. Stomach and digestive ailments give rise to dreams about disputes, while warnings of liver disease presented as green and yellow objects. These are the colours of bile, a product of the liver. Anaemia was said to cause feelings of suffocation and weakness, again a representation of the physical symptoms.

These interpretations are unreliable indicators of ill health but, knowing that our bodies do 'speak' to us in ways other than through pain, it would be advisable to consult a doctor, should dreams of this nature persist.

False Awakenings

Dreams are memories so in retrospect it is often difficult to be certain if an event really occurred or if it was a dream. One woman was so convinced that she had left her handbag on a train that she even telephoned the lost property office to enquire if it had been found. She was most relieved six months later when she found the handbag at the bottom of her wardrobe; she was also most perplexed when she realised it had been a bad dream and not reality.

Another example of a dream mistaken for reality is when we believe we are awake in the middle of the night, and see a person or ghost standing by the bed. Whoever it is we see is so real, and the memory so clear, that in the morning it is impossible to convince the dreamer that what occurred was actually a dream, and not a visitation. Dreams such as this are known as 'false awakenings' and account for many of the ghosts seen at night. But since we do not know everything there is to know about the dream state, who can say that the visitation did not take place, albeit in a way different to what we assume is normal? 'Things that go bump in the night' and other strange, unaccountable noises are also heard during false awakenings.

A Dream Within a Dream

Just as we sometimes dream we are awake, conversely we can dream we are asleep and dreaming. This produces a dream within a dream. One explanation is that in such dreams we reach deeper levels of awareness, but since these dreams are often of a mundane nature, apparently of little significance and no more revealing than other dreams, there is no evidence to support this theory. The point of them may, therefore, simply be to emphasise the necessity of looking deeply into certain problems and situations.

Falling

Falling through space is a sensation we often experience soon after 'falling asleep' or 'dropping off' to sleep. It is thought to be the feeling of transition from the awake state to that of sleep. The feeling of unexpectedly *stepping off a curb* followed by waking abruptly is a similar light, or early, sleep experience. Again, this is not a dream but is due to the sudden contraction of the muscles in our arms and, in particular, our legs. This is known as a 'myoclonic jerk', and a spasm of this nature is precisely what does occur should we inadvertently step off a curb. Not surprisingly, our unconscious associates this with the real thing and so incorporates it into a dream event, so that it seems that we are, for example, falling through space or dropping down a well.

There are also 'falling' dreams which occur long after we have fallen asleep. Our dreaming mind creates these for a purpose. Not surprisingly, they offer a message telling us that we fear we are 'falling from grace', 'being dropped', 'will fall upon hard times' or have to go through an ordeal that will 'bring us down'. There is an old wives tale associated with this dream which says that if you reach the bottom you will die. This is not true. Many have landed safely but we do usually wake up before we get there.

Being Chased

The feeling of *being chased* by someone or something, yet unable to run away or move, is also associated with the muscles in our limbs. During certain phases of sleep, in particular REM sleep, we are in fact *paralysed*. As with the myoclonic jerk, our unconscious awareness of not being able to move is often transformed into a scene in which we are rooted to the spot and cannot get away from whatever it is that is pursuing us. Sometimes the pursuer represents an aspect of the dreamer's own hostile tendencies, and sometimes it is the hostile tendencies of others. If, however, we can consciously identify the thing that chases us during the night, and can turn to face it during the day, it will no longer haunt our consciousness or our unconscious.

Walking and Talking in our Sleep

Sleep walking, known too as somnambulism, is an attempt to externalise a dream by putting it into action. Children do this far more than adults, probably because they are less inhibited and more agile. Most of us grow out of the habit but if an occasion arises which is severely distressing, we may, like Shakespeare's Lady Macbeth, actively express the nightmare in this way.

Talking in our sleep is similar, in cause, to sleep walking. It is an attempt to consciously express a dream verbally. It is possible to carry on a conversation with a sleeping person who is inclined to talk in their sleep, and to receive replies, but these are sometimes unintelligible.

When we are under mental pressure or we are not well physically we are more likely to sleep walk or talk. Most of the time we do not come to harm when we sleep walk but this is not always the case. Some somanbulists awake and find themselves in real danger, so it is a practice which should not be encouraged. Precautions should, therefore, be taken, especially where stairs and open windows are concerned.

Apnea

Apnea is a temporary cessation of breathing. New-born babies and young children frequently do this and it is alarming for those watching over them. The reason for this is that co-ordination between voluntary and involuntary responses in the body becomes temporarily dissociated. Holding on to the breath in this way causes carbon dioxide to build up in the blood and this, in turn, stimulates the respiratory system back into action, so normally there is no danger.

Premature babies are particularly prone to apnea and this is one reason why they are electronically monitored. If they should stop breathing, all that is necessary to make them breathe again is to push them gently. Fortunately, they soon grow out of this. It has, however, been suggested that some cot deaths may be due to apnea.

Breath-holding in sleep is less common in adults but if you have ever been alarmed when your sleeping partner holds his or her breath too long, do not worry unduly because it has probably continued since childhood. There are, however, some people who have to use a respirator at night, to make sure they do breathe, but fortunately such cases are rare.

Telepathy

Telepathic communication often takes place during dreams, usually spontaneously. It has been found that when we dream of someone we have not thought about for some time, there is a good chance that they have reciprocated and likewise dreamed of us. Two communicants do not necessarily have to be in harmony for this to happen, but telepathic links are more likely to occur when a close emotional relationship exists.

Sometimes a telepathic message is one of pain, fear and death. An example of this is the dreamer who awoke at 2am from a dream in which she saw her father holding his hand over his heart and at the same time felt a stabbing pain in her own chest. Next morning she telephoned her father's home and was told that he had died during the night from a heart attack. This happened at 2am, the precise moment she had the dream.

Experiencing pain or unpleasant events which do not relate directly to the dreamer is known as 'sympathetic dreaming'. Telepathic transference of a strong feeling or emotion is one explanation for those dreams which relate to the experiences of others. Such dreams are not prophetic; prophetic dreams reveal that which has not yet occurred.

Teleportation

Teleportation is projection to a distant bedside, where the dreamer in that bed actually sees the dream visitor standing there. This vision may be a false awakening or it may appear in a dream, but either way, evidence exists that this experience does take place. A mother who dreamed her daughter in Australia was seriously ill had this confirmed when she telephone her next morning. She also discovered that her daughter had seen her mother standing by the bedside. Her daughter had been asleep during the day so the times of the two dream experiences coincided exactly.

This phantom vision, the ghost of a living person, is known as a 'fetch'. Although most teleportations occur between those closely related, it is not always so. The experience of Tudor Pole, a well-known radio broadcaster, archaeologist, writer and philosopher in the 1930s, was a classic example. When excavating in Egypt he was taken ill with a severe fever. One night, as he restlessly dreamed, he thought he heard a tap on the cabin door. He awoke, or so he believed, and standing by his bed was a doctor dressed in a black cloak and wearing a top hat. The hat fascinated him because he could see right through it. The doctor placed this on a small table then proceeded to tell Tudor Pole that he was in practice in Britain but on some nights he travelled all over the world to visit those who needed his help. He then left, after giving the patient a special potion, which he drank. Next morning, Tudor Pole had recovered completely. The sequel to this was that when Tudor Pole returned to Britain, he appealed on BBC radio for this ghostly healer to come forward and, as a result, a Scottish doctor contacted him and confirmed that he did, in fact, travel during his sleep to those in need.

Flying

Flying dreams, known too as a form of astral projection, are experienced by seven out of ten people, at least once in their life. It is a most exhilarating feeling and few, if any, find it frightening. By using your arms like wings it is possible to rise above the ground and travel beyond the bedroom into the street, soar above the treetops and out into the country. It is even possible to be transported to faraway places and, as proof of this, bring back information that could not have been received in any other way. One explanation is that during sleep the spirit leaves the body. The practical belief is that such a dream reflects our inherited memory when, according to

Darwin's theory, our ancestors were birds. Psychologically, it is explained as a form of depersonalisation. These, however, are merely words to describe an experience none of us truly understands.

Whichever of these theories is correct, if indeed any, it still remains that there is a close link between flying dreams of this nature and teleportation. A further revelation is that a person who can fly in their sleep is rarely of a depressive nature. Symbolically, this makes sense because in reality flying dreams show that the dreamer wishes, or indeed is able to rise above his or her problems. They may also denote a desire to be free from a mundane situation that ties the dreamer to a life that is restrictive.

Sleep Learning

In the 1960s sleep was considered by many to be a waste of time so it was then the fashion to make use of these so-called 'lost hours' by learning a skill or foreign language. Those who introduced this believed that the brain had nothing better to do, so it would respond well to hypnotic suggestions. Sleep learning, as it was called, entailed listening to an instruction tape, while asleep, in order to acquire knowledge.

Results from this did not prove positive. Any facts learned in sleep faded from memory just as quickly as those learned when awake and, in addition to this, many who practised it found they could not concentrate during the day. Eventually, this form of learning was described as a form of brainwashing which deprived and inhibited spontaneous dreaming. It was, therefore, dropped.

Inspirational Dreams

It is well known that certain knowledge is acquired during sleep, but not in the way thought up by pragmatic educationalists. Many inventors, writers, statesmen, philosophers and musicians have their dreams to thank for the solution to a problem, the plot of a book or a concerto, but this information did not arrive as the result of sleep learning. It came to them spontaneously in dreams.

Professor Kekule

One inspirational dream that revolutionised the world was that of Fredrich August von Kekule, a professor of chemistry in Ghent a hundred years ago. He was having difficulty understanding the molecular structure of a certain substance when, one day, he dozed and had a dream. In this he saw atoms gambolling before his eyes. There were smaller groups which kept in the background, and in the foreground, with the acute vision peculiar to dreams, he distinguished larger structures forming strange configurations. These were in long chains, twisting and turning in snake-like fashion. Suddenly, he was astounded to see one 'snake' seize its own tail and mockingly form a circle. On waking it dawned on him that the circle formed by the snake symbolised the missing link in his researches. By transforming this scene into logic, he discovered it represented the ring theory underlying the constitution of benzene. In essence, he had discovered the complex mixture of hydrocarbons underlying the synthesis of petrol from oil.

Julius Caesar

It is said that Julius Caesar, a prolific dreamer, was guided by his dreams. On the strength of a dream, in which he violated his own mother, he decided to take his army across the Rubicon, a small river running along the Cisalpine border. The result of this was that he had in fact invaded his own motherland, an action that led to war between Caesar and the Senate.

He may well have acted upon his own dreams, but he disregarded those of others, in particular one his wife Calpurnia had. According to Shakespeare, her dream warned Caesar of 'the Ides of March'. If he had heeded this murderous portent, the tragedy would have been averted, and Calpurnia's dream would have remained a warning and not progressed into a prophecy.

William Shakespeare

Throughout the bard's work there are references to dreams and sleep and it has been said that, unless his works are viewed as if they were dreams, they make little sense.

The Tempest, set in that state between reality and illusion, is an example of this. Caliban dreams that 'the isle is full of noises and sounds and sweet airs that give delight and hurt not', and he cries to dream again. And the wise character of Prospero suggests that maybe life is but a dream anyway. 'We are', he says, 'such stuff as dreams are made of and our life is rounded with a little sleep'. The tragedy of *Macbeth* is a nightmare in itself and the sleep-walking Lady Macbeth re-enacts her crimes, agonising in her guilt. From *Hamlet*, the now famous line, 'To sleep, to sleep, perchance to dream', gave rise to a musical play, while the remainder of that quotation, 'For in that sleep of death what dream may come when we have shuffled off this mortal coil', offers an enlightened view of life after death. *A Midsummer Night's Dream* is but a dream inhabited by timeless images from real life, shadowy figures and figments from another dimension. In this we can identify with either and both worlds, but usually it is the symbolic one that wins.

The World of Dreams

Experiences in sleep are many and varied. We know that certain physiological changes are often incorporated into a dream and that false awakenings are difficult to distinguish from the true awake state. Flying and travelling in sleep may not be dreams at all, but a form of astral projection, just as inspirations which come in the dead of night are messages from a source beyond our reach in the harsh light of day. We do not know if dreams are a cause in themselves, or if they are reflections from outer consciousness, but either way, experiences in sleep cast a new light on our very existence.

CHAPTER FOUR

THE POWER OF DREAMS

Dreams, transient, intangible and elusive though they are, have the power to mould the destiny not only of the dreamer, but of nations as well. It is no exaggeration to say that the course of history itself has been changed more than once by a dream. In addition to Caesar's dream mentioned earlier (in which he attacked his own mother, an action he interpreted as a sign telling him to invade his motherland) there are other dreams from long ago which had even more lasting effects.

Most of us are familiar with biblical dreams and, in particular, the Pharaoh's dream of the seven fat kine (cattle) and seven full ears of corn. Egyptian Pharaohs and kings were great respecters of dreams. They saw them as guiding messages from their gods and goddesses and centuries before this Pharaoh had his dreams, there were in Egypt special temples and shrines dedicated to the art of dreaming.

The Dream Interpretations of Joseph

Imhotep of Memphis

Memphis was an early capital of ancient Egypt. It stood on the west bank of the Nile, south of present-day Cairo. Here was a great complex known to the Greeks centuries later as the Asclepion of Memphis. The Greeks identified their own god Asclepius with the Egyptian god Imhotep, so this place was, in fact, the shrine of Imhotep of Memphis.

At Memphis there were temples dedicated to the deities and Imhotep's, in particular, was dedicated to dreaming. Dreams were seen as oracles in themselves so those in need of help came here to receive divine guidance, inspiration, direction or peace of mind. This practice was once wide-spread not only in Egypt but throughout the world, where similar shrines existed.

The Butler's and the Baker's Dreams

When the Pharaoh had his famous dreams, Imhotep's temple had long since been silent. Nevertheless, the power, influence and effect of those dreams on the land of Egypt then, and on the rest of the world ever since, actually began before Pharaoh had his dreams. It began when Joseph interpreted the dreams of his two fellow prisoners.

Joseph, as the Bible says, was imprisoned on the Pharaoh's orders. The place of his imprisonment had originally been part of Imhotep's ancient shrine, possibly the temple of dreams itself, and it was here, not surprisingly, that the butler and baker had their dreams; forerunners to those of the Pharaoh. According to an early writer and explorer there was, in around AD900, a statue in the cavern where Joseph and the Pharaoh's butler and baker had been held captive. This statue was that of a seated figure with a parchment or open book on his lap. This figure was believed by the writer to be Joseph. There is, however, a statue from this part of Egypt which can be seen in the Louvre, Paris. It is of a seated figure with a scroll on his knees. This is said to be Imhotep, so the two statues may in fact be one and the same.

Bread and Wine

Remembering that the prison holding the three inmates was once a sacred shrine dedicated to the ancient gods of Egypt, it is not surprising that the Pharaoh's servants experienced such prophetic dreams. These dreams, related in Genesis 40:5–19 are as follows:

'And they dreamed a dream both of them, the butler and the baker of the King of Egypt, which were bound in prison. And Joseph saw them in the morning and they were sad and he asked "Whereof look you so sad today?" And they told him, "We dreamed a dream and there was no interpreter." And Joseph said to them, "Do not interpretations belong to God? Tell me them, I pray you." The butler told his dream to Joseph saying, "In my dream, behold, a vine was before me, with three branches, and it budded and blossom shot forth and the clusters brought forth ripe grapes. And Pharaoh's cup was in my hand and I took grapes and pressed them into his cup and gave it into Pharaoh's hand." "The three branches", said Joseph to the butler, "are three days; within three days Pharaoh will restore you to his service. And when he does, make mention of me, Joseph, and bring me out of prison." When the baker heard the interpretation was good, he too asked Joseph for the meaning of his dream, also featuring the number three. "Behold," he said, "I had three white baskets on my head. In the uppermost one was baked bread and sweetmeats for Pharaoh and the birds did peck and eat this." And Joseph answered: "The three baskets are three days, yet within three days will Pharaoh hang thee on a tree and the birds shall eat thy flesh."'

The Pharaoh's Dreams

All this came to pass; the butler returned to Pharaoh's service, and the baker was hanged within three days. Joseph, however, remained in prison, forgotten. Two years later the Pharaoh had two consecutive dreams which none of his advisers could understand. It was then that the butler remembered Joseph and how he had correctly interpreted his dream and that of the baker.

When the Pharaoh heard this he called for Joseph and, according to Genesis 41:1–7, related his dreams as follows: 'Behold, I stood on the river bank and there rose up out of the river seven fat kine; they fed in a meadow. And behold seven other kine followed them, poor and very ill-favoured and lean fleshed, much as I had never seen in Egypt. And the ill-famed did eat up the fat kine.' After this dream the Pharaoh awoke for a time and then, returning to sleep had another dream. 'And I saw in my dream, seven ears of corn on one stalk, full and good. And behold, seven ears, withered thin and blasted with the east wind, sprung up after them. And the thin ears devoured the seven good ears.'

Interpretation and Effect

Joseph's prophetic interpretation of these dreams is well known — seven years of plenty followed by seven years of famine. What is not so well known is that these two simple dreams, with different signs and scenes but with the same meaning, had the power to affect the course of history for ever more. Conjectual though it may be, if the butler and baker had not had their dreams, and if the Pharaoh had not had his, then Joseph would have remained in prison. Should he have remained there, there would have been no preparation for the famine which was soon to descend upon the land, so there would have been no corn in Egypt. It was, of course, this corn that brought Joseph's eleven brothers and his father Jacob down to Egypt, an event that led to the reuniting of Joseph with his father, Jacob, and those brothers who had abandoned him in the desert some years previously.

It was, therefore, symbolic dreams of the simplest yet most profound nature that set in motion a causal chain that is, through action and reaction, continuing to this day. As the Bible historically relates, after Joseph's reunification with his family they settled peacefully in Egypt and there the Twelve Tribes of Israel were born.

This was followed by the Exodus, the finding of the Promised Land, the tracing of David's line down to Mary, the birth of Jesus Christ and the rise of Christianity.

For the last 2000 years most of the wars that interfered with individual lives and nations were, rightly or wrongly, religious wars. Seen in this context, the present turmoil in Northern Ireland is the latest effect on the end of that causal chain started so long ago by the prophetic yet unobtrusive dreams of a Pharaoh whose significance and name have long since been forgotten.

Hitler's Dream

The dream Adolf Hitler is said to have experienced during the First World War certainly altered the course of history. Apparently he was sleeping in a bunker with many other war-wearied soldiers in 1917, when he had a most disturbing nightmare. In this, debris and molten earth fell upon him, crushing and suffocating him. He awoke in a terrible fright and ran outside into the cold night air, thankful that it had all been a bad dream. As he stood there, a shell hit the bunker, killing every sleeping occupant. To Hitler, this was divine providence. God, he believed, had saved him to save the Fatherland. The Second World War was, therefore, an indirect result of that dream, showing yet again the effective power they can have on the whole of humanity.

World Leaders and Their Dreams

Who can say that there are not many more dreams of the famous and infamous that have, unbeknown to us, affected our lives?

Long before Hitler, **Alexander The Great** acted upon one such fantasy which led to conquest, empire-building and great cost of human life. In this dream he saw a satyros — a nature spirit —

dancing on his shield. His personal dream interpreter named Aristander translated this as a word-picture indicating that Tyros was his for the taking. Until then, attacks on this city had proved disastrous but belief in his dream message urged him to try again. The result was that this time the city surrendered.

Joan of Arc's dreams convinced her that she was to be the saviour of France. From these, she contrived original schemes which persuaded the Dauphin that she was indeed capable of such victories. In G. B. Shaw's play *St Joan*, she is accused of listening to imaginary voices in her dreams. To this she replies: 'Of course, that is how messages of God do come.' For proof of this she could have referred her interrogators to the biblical text found in Job 33:14–16 which says: 'For God speaketh once, yea twice, yet man perceiveth it not. In a dream, in a vision of the night when deep sleep falleth upon slumbering men upon their bed, then He openeth their ears and sealeth in their instructions.'

Both **Napoleon** and **Bismark** were over-confident men. This boldness was due, in part, to their dreams, for in these they saw themselves as national heroes.

Napoleon, like Joan of Arc, saw himself as yet another saviour of France. In his dreams he planned his future military campaigns and on waking he would re-enact them in a sandpit full of toy soldiers. These represented the French army and their enemies. In the end, his dreams did not come true but many of his victories, it is said, were foreseen in this way.

Bismark was only six years old when Napoleon died but by then he was already showing signs of a very dominant character. During childhood he discovered that many of his dreams came true. These prophetic dreams continued, especially at the height of his military career. One such dream encouraged him to write to Emperor William, as follows:

'Your majesty's communication encouraged me to relate a dream
I had in the Spring of 1863, during the worst of the days of
struggle. I dreamed that I was riding on a narrow Alpine path, a

precipice on my right and rocks on my left. The path grew narrower and narrower so that my horse refused to proceed and it was impossible to turn round to dismount. Then, with my whip in my hand I struck the smooth rock and called on God. The whip grew to an enormous length, the rocky wall dropped like a piece of stage scenery and opened out into a broad path with a view over the hills and forest like a landscape in Bohemia: there were Prussian troops with banners and even in my dream the thought came to me that I must report it to your majesty.'

It was this dream that encouraged Bismark to stick to his policies which succeeded in Prussia taking over the leadership of the German federation, a step that led to Hitler's Fatherland.

Collective Dream Power

The sharing of dreams in the past was practised by many. The Indians of North America still use the collective power of their dreams to solve their community problems. At one time they held Dream Festivals lasting several days and the purpose of these was to encourage everyone taking part to dream about a particular issue. Concentrating beforehand on this issue, they would then sleep on it and pool their experiences in the morning. A distinct pattern always emerged and it was upon this that they formulated their future policies.

The indigenous people of New Zealand and Australia also pay attention to their dreams, especially relating them to the community as a whole. And so too do the Temiar Tribe in Malaysia. These non-violent, self-reliant people have intrigued the restless westerner ever since they were discovered in 1931. The secret of their balanced community was based on a code of practice saying that 'Where a man has given his labour he has a share of the harvest, though each man receives not in proportion to his skill and labour, but according to his needs.'

This was the very essence of Karl Marx's dream — every man

working to his full ability and taking according to his needs. In the civilised world it is impossible to achieve this dream of perfection, which is not surprising since most inhabitants of the so-called civilised world have not yet learned to dream together, let alone work together.

Corsica

There is, however, one place in Europe where collective dreaming still takes place, and this is in Corsica. Villagers who run their own affairs do this with the help of their dreams. As of old, they first concentrate on the problem, then dream about it. Next morning, many have similar dreams relating to that which they need to understand. Without knowing anything about this custom, many holiday-makers on the island have discovered that, on waking, the whole family had very similar dreams. It is as if a collective psyche takes over in the night and telepathically transmits a particular scene to those sleeping nearby, and then each person dreams of this in their own way.

Individual Dream Power

Today, few of us act on the advice of our dreams, yet just as they can affect history in a powerful way and give collective advice, so too can they alter the course of our life, even though we may not realise it consciously. It is possible that many decisions are made following a dream that is not even remembered but, more often than not, a personal dream can influence a chain of actions and reactions. This may not have world-shattering repercussions but it can certainly alter, or fulfil, one's destiny.

An example of this is the lonely bachelor who dreamed he was searching for his umbrella. On waking, he noticed it was pouring with rain, an event that reminded him of his dream. On the strength of this, he began to look for his umbrella but could not find it. Suddenly he remembered he had left it at his friend's house nearby, so he decided to call there to collect it on his way to work. His friend was not there but his sister was. She rarely visited her brother and, if it had not been raining, she would have left earlier, but decided to wait until the rain stopped. To cut a long story short, the dreamer retrieved his umbrella, escorted his friend's sister to the station, made arrangements to see her again, married her a year later and now has three children.

Inspiration and Originality

Dreams have always had the ability to provide the individual with creative and original ideas. Many writers, inventors and scientists have all been helped in this way. Sometimes this help comes in response to a request, as in the case of the novelist who was having a problem deciding on the title for her latest book. Before going to sleep she asked for a dream which would give her this; on waking, all she could remember was a large white flower with a bright yellow centre — a daisy. *Daisy* became a best-seller.

Sometimes dreams offer solutions spontaneously, and can be seen as an extension of logical, daytime thinking, even though they manifest symbolically or metaphorically. An example of this is Elias Howe, the inventor who reached the stage of extreme frustration when he could not complete his invention. He dreamed of Africans throwing spears, in particular noting that each spear had an eye-shaped hole at its tip. When he awoke, he instantly knew the answer to his problem. For weeks he had wondered where he should put the hole in the needle in his latest invention, which was the sewing machine.

Otto Loewi, the Nobel prize-winning biologist who discovered the theory underlying the chemical transmission of nerve impulses, saw all this in a dream. In fact, the professor had worked on this eighteen years previously but had forgotten all about it until it was retrieved from his memory and shown to him again in his dream.

The creative inspiration or answers that come to us in dreams are always linked to a personal quest or something that preoccupies us in our waking life. Unless we are working on an invention, as were Elias Howe and the biologist, solutions indicating the obvious yet elusive answers would be meaningless. Such inspiration is sometimes a projection of inner knowledge, wisdom and understanding, recognised unconsciously, but not consciously. There again, revelations do come out of the blue, offering undisputed originality.

Leonardo Da Vinci

Probably the greatest genius the world has known was 'the man who knew everything'; Leonardo da Vinci. An outstanding figure not only of the Renaissance, but before and since that time, he was an artist of rare power, and a pioneering scientist as well. His explorations were as diverse as anatomy, botany, geology, meteorology, physics, mathematics, geometry and music. His architectural drawings explored design problems in buildings, harbours, irrigation systems and canals, and his inventions were futuristic to say the least. These included sketches of submarines, diving suits, tanks, parachutes, flying machines, machine guns and cluster bombs, all at least four hundred years before their time.

A genius is a visionary, and a visionary is a dreamer — but not all dreamers are visionaries. The difference between the two is that the genius da Vincis of the world can pluck an idea that comes to them in the still of the night and, from it, create reality. To them, the real world is the inner world and all wisdom relating to the outer world comes from here. But above all, a genius differs from others because he or she is a good listener, not to those around them, but to their own quiet voice which speaks to them within.

Spiritual Rector — Personal Counsellor

Our inner voice never speaks to us louder or clearer than in our dreams. If we do not hear this voice or enter into a dialogue, albeit in metaphorical terms, then we are ignoring a source of immense guidance. C.G. Jung was so impressed with the personal inner cradle of knowledge and wisdom that he used to say that it acted as a spiritual rector and personal counsellor, who introduced a balancing force that counteracted the one-sidedness and extreme attitudes of the conscious mind.

Many of our problems concern personal relationships. People may offer advice, but since they cannot possibly know the truth, the fears and the hopes that we alone know, they are, compared with our inner counsellor, only partially helpful. Unless they say what we want to hear, we ignore them, but when we say such things to ourself, we cannot afford not to listen, and take note. Common sense tells us that there is no living being who knows us like we know ourselves, just as no other person can digest our food for us, nor can they solve our problems or make our decisions. Our untapped potential that often reveals itself in our dreams is more than capable of supporting us in our every need. For proof, we have only to look back in history to realise the influence and the power dreams have in this respect.

The Incubation of Dreams

To contact our creative dreaming mind and elicit help from it, we have to ask for the right dream, at the right time. In the days when dreams were looked upon as oracles and interpretations were regarded as a form of divination, the ancient races 'incubated' their dreams. This simply means they requested a dream that would show them the way ahead, give them comfort or even heal them.

The word 'incubation' derives from the Latin 'incubare' meaning 'to lie down upon'. Today, we associate this word with the hatching of eggs, when in fact it originally meant the hatching or production of fertile dreams. To incubate a dream centuries ago it was necessary to visit a special shrine such as those still to be seen today in Egypt and in Greece. There, dreamers spent several days in ritualistic preparation involving fasting and relaxing. When the time came to incubate their dream they would lie down and sleep in the temple in readiness for a nocturnal visit from the appropriate god, goddess, angel or divine messenger who would dispense help.

Classical literature is rich in examples of communication between man and his gods. At Delphi, the shrine of Apollo and the temple of Epidauros were two places to which pilgrims journeyed in search of help, and it was here too that the sick went, in hope of a divine cure. Philosophers tried hard to explain the mysteries of sleep in physical terms, but all failed. Although Greek sages studied the cause of dreams, the public were only interested in what their dreams could offer them, and what they meant. We are still no nearer knowing the motivating mechanism behind them, but like the dreamers of old, it is the personal messages they convey that interest us most of all.

Incubation Today

Today there are no shrines dedicated to Morpheus, the god of dreams, nor to Hypnos, the god of sleep, but this does not mean their powers have deserted us. They, as universal, archetypal principles, are still ready and waiting, but they are rarely summoned to do our bidding. Nor are we without oracles — our own dreaming mind is precisely this.

In present-day language, the incubation of dreams means asking ourselves for a dream relating to a particular problem. The gods still play a part in this for the process begins with sleep — Hypnos's influence, followed by a special dream — Morpheus's response. The way in which you incubate your dreams depends on your beliefs and understanding of yourself and the world around you. If your belief is that God provides your answers, then make your request in the form of an invocative prayer. If, on the other hand, you believe that God helps those who help themselves, then make your request directly to that aspect of yourself whom you know is capable of contacting forces of great power and wisdom.

The most important aspect of incubating a dream is its conciseness. This means you must put your question and request as clearly as possible. Rambling requests receive rambling responses, so the simpler and more succinct the request, the simpler and more succinct will be the response. If your request is to be in the form of a prayer, the following lines may be helpful as a format:

'Almighty God, from whom all good things come, please send me a dream to show me how to accept the present situation/help me to understand the problem/make me well again/know what to do next. I shall accept your advice and act upon it accordingly. Thank you, God. Amen.'

If you decide to make a direct approach to yourself, the following more authoritative lines are suggested as a basis for your positive affirmation:

'Dreaming mind, please send me tonight a clear dream to show me precisely how to accept the present situation/help me understand the problem/know what to do next. I am ready and waiting to receive helpful information and I will act upon such advice in the future. Thank you, dreaming mind.'

A further suggestion is that you write out your prayer or affirmation beforehand, thus making a permanent record of it and finally, be sure to write down all you can remember from your dreams, when you wake next morning.

CHAPTER FIVE

PSYCHOLOGICAL DEFINITIONS OF DREAMS

During the nineteenth and the first half of the twentieth century dreams were regarded mainly as psychological statements. These were said to arise from personal fears, inhibitions, attitudes and unfulfilled hopes. Dreams which did not fit these definitions, such as those which came true or gave inspirational solutions and ideas, were dismissed as mere coincidences, or the result of logical deduction.

The intellectual approach to dreams began with the Greek philosophers. Since the dawn of time the mysteries of the mind have intrigued humanity and even today, despite numerous anatomical and physiological discoveries, the question, as Shakespeare put it, 'What is this stuff of dreams?' still remains. Intellectual philosophers believed our senses — seeing, hearing, touching, smelling and tasting — often deceived us, and when they did, our dreams tried to show us our mistakes. It was **Plato** who gave us the word **ideas**. These were certain qualities or essences of the mind which he saw as realities. Among these he cited beauty, truth, faith, hope and all abstract thoughts, and it was these abstract thoughts that filled our dreams.

Plato's pupil, **Aristotle**, had a different view from that of his master. He believed the body to be inhabited by a soul which has three different aspects — the nutritive, the sensitive and the reasonable. The *nutritive* soul keeps the body alive; the *sensitive* soul feels emotions and sensations and is the seat of memory; the *reasonable* soul thinks, judges and reasons. Together, these three aspects form *the mind.*

In Plato's *Republic,* its writer says, 'In all of us, even in good men, there is a lawless, wild beast which peers out at us in sleep', thus showing that the seeds of the psychological approach were sown long before Freud tracked down Habitual Complexes and other disturbing inner conflicts. Since that time, 'mind' has been bandied about to such an extent that even now it is still only a word for something we do not fully understand. Even Freud and his pupil Jung, the two greatest psychologists to date, could not agree on a common definition of the word. They did, however, leave us with psychological language relating to the realm of the mind and dreams.

At the beginning of this century there were two schools of experimental psychology. One originated in America and was known as 'Behaviourism', the other was the German Gestalt school. Behaviourists believed that the study of human actions and reaction revealed the reasons for behaviour and mental processes. On the other hand, Gestalt psychologists concentrated on perception, believing that we perceive the whole before we perceive the parts. An example of this is that we learn a tune before we learn the notes, or we see a rose in totality before looking at each petal. These two schools still exist today and although each studies human psychology in different ways, they blend in many respects. Both are concerned with the workings of the conscious mind, whereas Freud and Jung were more occupied with unconscious awareness.

Sigmund Freud (1856-1939)

Sigmund Freud was the originator of *psychoanalysis.* This began with the belief that the mind acted as a censor which had the ability to alter a disturbing dream into one which would not affect sleep. Having studied hypnosis he also came to the conclusion that emotions and subconscious motivations were the prime movers in our lives, rather than intelligence. This, plus his belief in the importance of infantile sexuality in the development of the personality, offended most of his colleagues.

Repression and Sex Drive

Freud believed that most people reject hostile and destructive impulses, as well as socially unacceptable forms of sexual enjoyment. These urges are not acknowledged by the conscious self so arouse anxiety which in turn blocks such negative feelings. This process he called *repression*.

This theory was followed by Freud's beliefs on human sexuality. The sexual instinct he called *libido*, an urge that is present from birth. It could, he thought, be satisfied in many ways, from active sport to artistic creativity and it is often repressed because of demands made on the individual by society. It is this that creates conflict within the personality. To Freud, the sexual instinct was the major driving force; the second drive he saw as self-preservation. These two drives he combined into one urge — 'the life instinct' which he called *eros*.

Id, Ego and Superego

The backbone of Freudian psychology is formed by three closely interrelated aspects of the human personality: the *id*, the *ego* and the *superego*.

The id is the name he gave to the subconscious mind. This is made up of primitive urges and instincts and seeks gratification without ethical control and without considering the consequences. The ego is the conscious part of the personality. It stands between the id and reality, and acts as a sort of mediator. The superego is partly conscious and urges the individual to resist negative impulses of the id. It contains 'high ideals' and acts as the conscience, so judges between good and bad behaviour.

Dreams and the Subconscious

Repressed impulses of the id and the superego strive for expression, thus exerting pressure on the personality. These, according to Freud, surface in slips of the tongue, and in dreams. Freud soon realised that dreams gave him invaluable clues leading to repressed feelings which, in turn, caused psychological disorders. These clues were symbolic in essence because they represent a submerged wish that is socially taboo or too frightening to be allowed to surface, not only consciously, but even overtly as a dream.

Free Association

Initially, Freud used hypnosis but soon found this to be inadequate. Some patients simply could not be hypnotised and those who were did not always respond to his commands and suggestions. This led him to seek an alternative in the form of *free association of ideas*. By relaxing on a couch and saying the first thing that came into their minds, he found that a succession of ramblings revealed the source of his patients' mental anxieties and neuroses.

Free association of ideas may have been the origin of psychoanalysis but dreams remained Freud's main source of information on hidden, forbidden fears and anxieties. In 1900 he published his classic work *The Interpretation of Dreams*.

Carl Gustav Jung (1875-1961)

Carl Gustav Jung was Freud's pupil. Although sharing some of his beliefs, Jung soon parted company with Freud mainly because of the latter's emphasis on sexuality and the too materialistic and biological orientation of his theories. Jung's overall doctrine, eventually known as *analytical psychology*, is deeply influenced by myths, mysticism, metaphysics and religious experience. This, he believed, accounted for the spiritual nature in man whereas Freud's theories dealt mainly with mundane encounters.

Jung redefined many psychological terms used at that time, in particular those of Freud. Ego, for example, he saw as a complex situated at the centre of consciousness — the *me*. Another Freudian term he redefined was libido. To Jung this signified not only sexual energy, but all the energetic processes of life, from sexual activity to the process of healing. The id, ego and superego were terms Jung never used. Instead, he used *consciousness, personal unconscious* and the *collective unconscious*. Consciousness and personal unconsciousness partially compare with the id and the ego but there is a considerable difference between Freud's superego and Jung's collective unconscious. This, Jung believed, is the largest and deepest area of the psyche. It contains the roots of the four psychological functions: sensation; intuition; thought; and feeling. It also contains inherited racial, ancestral and historic memories.

Archetypes and Autonomous Complexes

In Jungian psychology it is accepted that the collective unconscious consists of basic components of the human psyche which Jung called *archetypes*. This is a universal concept containing a large element of myth. The concept of archetypes is very important in the understanding of dream symbology for it explains why some dreams have a universal meaning which applies to everyone, and why others are purely personal and concern the dreamer only. Jung saw the archetype as an *autonomous complex*, that is, a part of the psyche that detaches itself and appears to be independent from the rest of the personality.

The Persona

The more personal autonomous complexes or archetypes were seen by Jung to be part of the psyche. He called these the *persona*, the *shadow*, the *anima* and the *animus*, and it is these that appear in dreams in the form of figures which may or may not be recognised by the dreamer.

The persona is the face the individual presents to the rest of the world. It is the conscious personality, identifiable with Freud's ego. In dreams it appears in the form of a figure which typifies the me in certain circumstances. Sometimes it will be a stern old man, a wise woman, a rakish lout, a clown or a child. It is an attitude of the dreaming mind. Sometimes extremes of this will be counterbalanced in a dream by a character playing an opposite role. For example, the person who presents to the world an overtly moral and conservative face may well dream of a rogue, or conversely, the rogue may dream of angels.

The Shadow

The strong side of an individual's personality usually dominates the whole persona. The weaker aspects are then left in the background where they form into the shadow self and it is this, another autonomous complex or archetype, that surfaces on occasions in dreams. Sometimes instincts and urges are embodied in the shadow, along with negative and destructive feelings generally. This can be a threatening figure in the guise of someone disliked by the dreamer who acts out a special role between the shadow and conscious self. This is exemplified by the struggle between Dr Jekyll and Mr Hyde in Robert Louis Stevenson's novel.

One way to recognise the shadow figure in a dream is to observe your most negative reactions and feelings about certain people and circumstances, for it is the things we dislike most that form the core of the shadow self.

Anima and Animus

The anima and the animus are terms Jung invented to describe those characteristics of the opposite sex which exist in every man and woman. The anima is the hidden female in men. The animus is the hidden male in women.

The anima is the centre of the compassionate, emotional, instinctive and intuitive side of the male personality. This archetype is a collective form of all the women a man has known in his life, especially his mother. The integration of this into his personality allows a man to develop the sensitive side of his nature thus allowing him to become a less aggressive, more generous, warm and understanding individual. Denial or repression of the anima results in obstinacy, hardness, rigidity and even emotional and physical cruelty.

The animus is the centre of the practical, independent, self-assured and risk-taking side of the female personality. As an archetype, it is a collective form of all the men a woman has known in her life, in particular her father. It is the integration of this into her nature that allows her to become a leader, good organiser and bread-winner, but when a woman ignores these aspects within herself she becomes whining, fretful and insecure.

Coming to terms with this archetype allows men and women to have a better understanding of the opposite sex. This also enables them to extend and develop their capabilities more fully. The emergence of the anima or animus in one's dreams indicates the integration of the personality. This integration Jung called the *individuation process*.

The Higher Self

The self as an archetype represents the idealistic and spiritual nature of men and women. When this appears in dreams it usually indicates the individuation process has been completed. In a man's dream the self appears as the Wise Old Man. In a woman's dream the figure is that of the Great Mother. Each of these has four aspects which represent the four qualities of the psyche — intellect, emotion, practicality and intuition — but these qualities also have both a positive and a negative aspect.

	GREAT MOTHER *positive*	*negative*	GREAT FATHER *positive*	*negative*
INTELLECT	Mother	Terrible Mother	Father	Ogre
EMOTION	Princess	Seductress	Prince	Philanderer
PRACTICALITY	Amazonian	Huntress	Warrior	Dictator
INTUITION	Priestess	Witch	Priest	Black Magician

The four dual aspects of womanhood and manhood form the basic archetypal characteristic of the individual. Rarely does one aspect dominate completely, but when it does it is recognised as an eccentricity. A balance between the four positive qualities is what should be strived for, plus the recognition of the four opposite characteristics which may emerge under certain circumstances.

Symbolic Archetypal Figures

The figures in our dreams which represent our different qualities may themselves be symbolised by something else. For example, a spider with its husband-devouring nature may represent the negative aspect of mother and wifehood. Fairytales are another example, for their message can best be understood when interpreted as a dream. The Prince and Princess who live happily ever afterwards, Cinderella and Sleeping Beauty are all romantic qualities of the psyche. When looking for partners of the opposite sex, it is the images of these that masquerade in our sleep, thus providing us with the proverbial 'man and woman of our dreams'.

Such Stuff as Dreams are Made of

No two dreams are identical. Some follow mundane, logical patterns while others seem irrational and illogical. Others are symbolic and abstract yet others are as normal as waking life. They can be dull, exciting, frightening and enjoyable; they can fulfil our wishes or frustrate us.

Whatever this 'stuff of dreams' is, it seems real at the time. For all the investigations by Freud, Jung and others, and the psychological language they have invented to describe the various aspects of the psyche, dreams are as mysterious and elusive as ever they were. The following words from *The House of Fame*, written by Chaucer in the fourteenth century were true then and may ever remain so.

PSYCHOLOGICAL DEFINITIONS OF DREAMS

God turns to good all our dreams
For one great mystery, to me it seems,
Is how it is that dreams are born
Whether at evening or at morn,
And why it is that some come true,
While others never do.

Why that's a dream of things to come,
Why this is revelation,
Why this is nightmare, that a dreaming,
Never holds for all men the same meaning.
Why this is an apparition, why these are oracles,
I know not, but if the causes of these miracles
Are known by someone better than I
Let him explain them . . .

CHAPTER SIX

THE LANGUAGE OF DREAMS

The language of dreams is the language of the unconscious — a psychological text which conveys messages in a very different way to words and speech. Instead of these it uses scenes, signs and symbols, so to understand them we have to learn their language. Some of the scenes are literal but others are symbolic, in the form of word-pictures. It is these that are more difficult to interpret and are usually dismissed as nonsense when in fact they may be most profound. Once we know dreams have to be viewed in this way, they will soon begin to make sense.

When we are awake our thinking is based mainly on conscious impressions, but during sleep our dreams combine these with deeper unconscious images, thus producing a layered communication. This accounts for the fact that some dreams are literal, simply re-enacting stored conscious memories, whilst others are symbolic, and still others are a mixture of both.

Primary — Not Primitive

Every thought is based on an image, and a series of images makes up a scene. Dream imagery arises not so much from outer stimuli —

although the sound of a telephone or door bell may well be incorporated into it — but from inner effects ranging from memories to psychic and spiritual influences which defy the logic of conscious reckoning. Imagery, whether in dreams or in the conscious awake state, was, until recently, considered to be a primitive, animal way of expressing, experiencing, assessing and processing information compared with speaking, writing and hearing. Now it is known to be the basis of all thought, speech and action. Without scenes in our head there is nothing. Imagery, therefore, is the *primary* way of thinking and being, not primitive, and it is imagery, some literal and some symbolic, that forms our dreams.

Head Versus Heart

Dreams reflect both the outer world and the inner. These relate to our head and our heart, our conscious reasoning and unconscious awareness. The logic of the head usually rules during the day whereas the instinctive feelings of the heart have their say at night. Although we do not often realise it, this duality allows us to view life and solve problems in two distinctly different ways: intellectually and intuitively.

'Sleep on it' is sound advice because this gives us the opportunity to consider a problem from an entirely different point of view — that of the heart. Even if we do not remember any of our dreams, we nonetheless feel better about things the next morning. This is because certain conclusions have been reached at the prime, unconscious level of understanding and this, in turn, brings about a change of attitude.

Literal Dreams

Although all dreams take place in our unconscious, and consist of imagery, not every dream is symbolic or metaphorical. Some are literal scenes. They are action replays of previous events and mirror exactly what has previously taken place. The reason for these dreams is that they give the dreamer the chance of having another look at a particular incident that either did not make sense at the time, or was misunderstood.

When awake our unconscious takes note of far more than we realise, so if our dreaming mind considers it would help to review an event, it conjures up images of past scenes as action replays. In addition to literally recreating an event, these dreams also offer objective assessment in that they do not favour the dreamer any more than they discriminate against an opponent.

Most literal dreams reflect the outer world with its practical problems and show how to deal with them intelligently on waking. If we do not realise a dream is purely literal we may fall into the trap of trying to read more into it than there is. A literal dream must, obviously, be taken literally; otherwise its message will be totally lost.

This type of dream can be upsetting when it is an action replay of an unhappy event. Although re-experiencing such a thing cannot alter a situation, we can still benefit from it in another way. Reliving memories of this nature is actually one way of coming to terms with what has happened. The loss of a job, of status or even of someone close to us are examples of the help given by these dreams. In contrast to the sad dream, there is the dream which re-enacts happy events from the past. This is not a sentimental, self-indulgent dream experience, although some may be of a compensatory nature. These dreams are produced by our unconscious in order to rekindle affection, make up for loneliness and even to recharge our sense of humour which will have the effect of making light of certain pressing problems. The agony and the ecstasy of sad and happy literal dreams are not intended to frustrate, nor to entertain. They are genuinely meant to inform, help and heal.

Biblical Example of Literal Dreams

Excellent examples of literal dreams can be found in the New Testament. In fact, most of the dreams in this part of the Bible are literal and give literal, practical messages. One of the best-documented accounts is given in Matthew 2: 11/12. Here we read how the three wise men took gifts to Bethlehem to give to the new-born King. Then in a dream one of them received the following warning: '"Return not to Herod"; and they departed for their country another way.'

A further example is found in the next verse which continues: 'And when they were departed an angel of the Lord appeared to Joseph in a dream saying "Arise and take the young child and his mother, and flee into Egypt and remain there until I bring you further word for Herod will seek the young child to destroy him."' When Herod was dead, Joseph received another dream as promised, telling him it was safe for him and his family to return to their native land.

These dreams did not have to be interpreted because their messages were self-explicit. What had to be done, however, was to heed the warnings and act upon the advice they gave. Although these dreams had a profound effect on the future history of the world (if Joseph had not had a dream telling him to go down into Egypt with Jesus and Mary it can be presumed that Jesus, along with many other innocent male babies, would have been a murder victim), most literal dreams affect just the dreamer. The most important feature about them is that their literal messages should be acted upon.

Symbolic Dreams

Many symbolic dreams are metaphorical and should be interpreted as such. They should be understood in the same way as the saying 'Out of the frying pan and into the fire' — a word-picture warning that someone is going from one bad situation to another.

Unfortunately, we have been prevented from investigating the language of dreams because its language is one of images, the basis of imagination. From school days, imagination is something that has not been encouraged. To be told you have a vivid imagination is usually a polite way of saying that you are lying, so it is not surprising society dictates that dreams, especially symbolic and archetypal dreams, are purely figments of our imagination. It is the translation of symbolic imagery into logical terms that causes the confusion but once it is recognised that we exist in two different worlds inhabited by our head and our heart, and that each has its own set of rules, references and languages, interpretations are, with a little practice, amazingly simple.

Our inner world is far less familiar to us than that of the outer world where words — written and spoken — are used to communicate with one another. The limitations surrounding this are considerable for there are many experiences which are quite impossible to convey in this way. For example, fear, love, anxiety, hope and hate are extremely difficult to put into words, but in the language of dreams, they can be expressed in a thousand and one different ways. Since symbolic dreams reflect feelings, deep emotions, intuition, inspiration and inner expressions which cannot easily be put into words; and since the language of dreams is representational (symbolic), it should not come as a surprise that they substitute one thing, and even one person, for another.

The Collective Unconscious

Most dreams of this nature are personal and relate to individual problems which we need to solve or understand. The symbolism our dreaming mind uses to do this is gathered from experiences and events encountered in the outer world but, in addition to these, there are those dreams which are far removed from everyday activity. These find their origin in what C.G. Jung called the *collective unconscious*. Symbols are archetypes from this realm have never before entered the dreamer's head.

It is the collective unconscious that gives rise to our more mystical dreams. In these we may meet a dragon, a snake, a mysterious beast, a giant or some beautiful being. In the waking state we tell ourselves such things belong to the land of myth but in sleep they take on real significance. This is because we realise in sleep that in the dream world we communicate with ourselves, not only in a symbolic language, but in archetypal imagery that finds its origin way back in the mists of time.

To dream of hidden treasure in a magic garden is not, therefore, a dream of wishful-thinking. It is a powerful message telling the dreamer that within oneself, within one's grasp, is a treasure beyond belief. This treasure appears to be gold, silver and jewels, but this is not the gold, silver and jewels we find for sale in shops. These treasures symbolise inner wealth and riches of the soul, things money can never buy.

Through the impossible dream we are shown far-reaching ideals which, if translated correctly, can be achieved. When this inner fantasy is related to personal, practical aims, it can bring about a previously inconceivable level of enthusiasm which, in some unfathomable way, brings about success. This, then, is the true magic of dreams — the marrying together of the heart and the head, inner symbolic guidance and outer, directive determination.

Collective Symbolism

Although every dream is unique there are certain actions, objects, people and scenes which make regular appearances in dreams. These are the collective symbols and, although they have the same overall meaning, their messages are different when applied to individual circumstances. For example, we all experience similar problems in life — domestic worries, difficulties with relationships, loss of an aim, frustrated ambition, etc., so it is not surprising that these are represented by similar imagery.

Many of us have, at some time or another, had the dream of being lost in an unfamiliar town, walking down unrecognisable streets. 'Where am I?' we each ask ourselves. Once we realise the dream is telling us we have 'lost our sense of direction', an expression often used metaphorically when awake, we can begin to act on the message and make plans leading to a destinational aim or goal.

Journeys

Most dreams have some form of movement or travel in them, denoting the dreamer's progress (or lack of it, depending on circumstances in the dream), as they make their way through life. Walking, running, skipping, cycling, riding a horse, driving a car, travelling by bus, train or boat, all symbolise the way the dreamer is forging ahead. Narrow byways and winding streets, crossroads, flyovers and underpasses, all represent that path fraught with encounters, potential hazards and the unexpected.

Stopping at stations, waiting for aeroplanes or buses, all reflect situations common to each of us. When viewed in the light of the collective unconscious and its language, it is not difficult to see that we are telling ourselves in these dreams that we have reached a stage, a staging post, where we must decide exactly where we are going next. Missing a boat, bus or train, has the metaphorical meaning of having missed the boat. Speeding in a car can, when viewed in this way, become a warning sign telling us to slow down and, similarly, when someone else is driving and we are a passenger, we know that, in reality, we are not in control of our own life.

Houses

Houses, flats, hotels and buildings appear in dreams more than any other object. Unless the dreamer is contemplating buying a house or is involved in the building trade, the house in a dream symbolises the dreamer. It is the *mansion of the soul*. Often we return to this night after night, where we find ourselves in different rooms and different parts of the house. These symbolise various aspects of our life, our interests and our characteristics.

A kitchen in a dream, for example, sets the scene before which domestic and family matters are enacted; a bedroom suggests more intimate things and the living room introduces social life and its encounters. Some rooms are mysteriously locked, others contain secrets and there are some emanating a distinct haunting feeling. Going up stairs in our dream house leads to towering ambitions, aims and hopes and, when we descend to the basement, we know that hidden fears and things we wish to keep out of sight and out of mind are stirring.

Water

Dreams of water are almost as common as dreams of houses. Water in a dream is a symbol of life itself — the water of life — so in this context its image conveys spiritual rebirth and cleansing. The first nine months of our existence are spent in water, so it is not surprising that we use this as a medium to express the 'fluid' side of our nature — emotions and feelings flowing from the heart.

We speak of 'getting into deep water' so, when life becomes complicated and we feel 'out of our depth', it is not uncommon to have a dream in which we are near drowning. A lake in a dream, however, suggests a special haven towards which we are struggling, but a flood of water warns of force beyond our control.

Teeth

The dream that teeth are loose and falling out usually occurs when changes are taking place in the dreamer's life. They are particularly frequent during adolescence and early adult life; times coinciding with leaving school and starting work. A change of job, getting married or divorced and even the anticipation of moving from one house to another is often sufficient to encourage such dreams.

The association between losing teeth in dreams and real-life events is the stage in life during which we lose our milk teeth. This signifies the change from childhood to adulthood, a time when responsibilities begin to descend upon us. In essence, these dreams reflect a fear associated with changes which may even be for the better, so the question of maturity or 'growing up', however old we may be, arises.

Snakes

Although we may dislike snakes when awake, they rarely horrify us in dreams. This is because they are acting out a symbolic role. In Freudian terms a snake is the inevitable sign of sexual activity, the sex urge, but it is far more than just this. Snakes have the power to represent the entire range of human energies, from physical pursuits which include sex, through ambitious drives, to the spiritual ability to heal. The ancients used snakes to portray healing forces, and today, the British Medical Association has a snake twined around a stick as its emblem.

Between the extremes the snake will act out the role of the 'viper in the bosom' and the 'snake in the grass', thus depicting deceit, cunning, underhand goings on and jealousies. When seen in a dream as a passive, large brown snake, however, it symbolises earthy stability leading to greater understanding and wisdom.

Collective Meaning — Personal Message

The majority of dreams have some element of collectivity in them by virtue of the fact that we are all human, share the same collective inheritance, society and history, and have similar problems. As well as this, there is also the unique symbolism of the individual which always overrides the collective. Personal feelings based on personal experiences alter the traditional meaning but, in addition to even this, there is the symbolism created by the individual as a result of their own experiences and associations.

Only when a collective meaning is applied to individual

circumstances and situations does it become a personal message. Interpreting dreams from this point of view is relatively easy because the traditional meanings have only to be applied to the dreamer's own circumstances to make sense. Dream dictionaries are useful in that they give collective meanings, but they do not give personal messages. In the final analysis, since dreamers create their own dreams they are, through the use of both collective and individual symbolism, the best, if not the only, capable interpreters.

CHAPTER SEVEN

UNDERSTANDING YOUR DREAMS

Understanding your dreams helps you to understand not only yourself, but others as well. Analysing them gives access to that inner world which is both personal and shared by everyone, and doing this is an imaginative and poetic experience. We are educated into attitudes and values related to logic and the outer world, a culture leaving little room for such things as dreams; yet without them there would be no logic.

An interpretation of a dream should lead to insight and possibly to action as a result. To arrive at this, we have to translate *unconscious imagery* into *conscious understanding*. There are many ways of doing this — from taking the message literally, as in literal dreams, to asking for another dream to reinforce or clarify its message. Dreams are layered with meaning, and each level is disguised or camouflaged. Some dreams have just one layer, with the meaning lying just beneath the surface. These can usually be understood by associating the dream with a particular incident. Others can only be decoded step by step.

A Request for Help

As we invent our own dreams using a combination of the collective language of dreams plus our own unique sign language, we can, therefore, incubate a dream; that is, we can ask ourselves for further details in a later dream. Although it appears we have little control over what we dream, requests made by our conscious self to our unconscious self are always fulfilled.

When a dream seems important, but impossible to understand, ask yourself just before going to sleep to send another which will give you further insight. If you can relate the dream to an incident or problem but cannot understand its message, think about this incident before making your request. Some dreams reflect the worry associated with problems, showing we are wasting too much time doing this, without trying to do something about it. Even insoluble problems can be helped by a change of attitude and acceptance — and this is where dreams can help.

Put your request either as a prayer or as a direct command to your dreaming mind. In your thoughts, state to yourself quite clearly what you want to know and tell yourself that in the morning you will remember all that you have dreamed. To show sincerity, place a notebook and pen by your bedside in readiness to write down the first thing that comes into your head — your dream. Sometimes it takes up to three or four requests, depending on the link between your inner and outer selves, but eventually your efforts will be well rewarded.

Lucid Dreams

Lucid dreaming is to know you are dreaming at the time of the dream. When a dream is very unusual we often say to ourselves, 'I must be dreaming'. When it is a particularly bad one, this realisation wakes us up but, in addition to this, there are three other important aspects associated with lucid dreaming. First, to become aware or awake in a dream shows we have discovered something new about ourselves. Secondly, having discovered this, and realise we alone have created the dream-scene, it is within our capability to alter that dream-scene. Thirdly, since many dreams do come true, it is possible to create a dream-scene that will do just this.

Not only do we forge a link between our outer and inner selves in lucid dreaming, but we can achieve a degree of control over our own lives. If, for example, we are not well, seeing ourselves healed in a dream can bring about recovery. Another example of self-help received in this way is using lucid dreaming as a dress rehearsal for life. If an important interview or meeting is to take place, to dream about it beforehand generates tremendous self-confidence.

The implications and applications of this are enormous. To achieve the best result lucid dreaming has to be linked with the incubation of dreams, namely requesting the right dream at the right time.

Warning Dreams

We do not dream for amusement nor about things in life that we can deal with when awake. This is why most dreams contain a warning message or at least a message concerning negative aspects. Again, understanding the message is only the first step — next we have to do something about the problem. A warning dream can all too easily turn into a prophetic dream. An example of this is the man who dreamed he was driving his car at great speed and had an accident. This was a literal warning clearly telling him to be careful and not to drive so fast but he ignored this and the inevitable happened. To him, the dream was prophetic but if he had acted on the advice it gave, there is no doubt that he would have saved himself from a bad experience.

Sometimes warning dreams relate to someone else. By telling those involved to be careful may avert trouble but unless they are a close relative, it is difficult to do this. A mother, whose son owned a red power boat, had a vivid dream showing him speeding in a blue boat that turned over, and drowned him. She was so upset by this that she begged him not to race but his reply was that his boat was red. The following Saturday he went as usual to the lake where he kept his boat and for some reason he drove his friend's boat. It was blue, and sadly, the dream came true.

Free Association

The manifest elements of a dream are, especially when it is a symbolic dream, the tip of the iceberg. Beneath the surface there is a network of interrelated dream symbolism even though the surface story is complete. Each of the images that go to make that story originate beneath the surface and each of these has their own personal or collective associations. It is, therefore, association between manifest images and past, apparently unrelated events, that is important.

We need to think of a dream and its associations as the first step towards interpretation. This approach — free association — gives much more information than simply working with the remembered part of your dream only. Having noted all you can remember about your night's dreaming as soon as possible after waking, associations can be made any time after that without loss of dream substance.

Free association is a point of departure from the surface dream. The more relaxed your attitude towards this, the easier it will be to make personal associations. Although this can be carried out at any time, a peaceful atmosphere without distractions is to be preferred. Think of your dream and allow yourself to daydream. It is often through linking surface images with deeper unconscious memories that critical triggers are discovered, and it is these that lead to the reason for the dream and eventually to its message. This is only a step in decoding a dream and is not an end in itself. There is also the temptation to pursue associations too far, a practice Jung found to be altogether distracting. If this happens, bring your attention back to the sign, symbol or object of departure and go over the first part of the chain of ideas flowing from this.

Ann's Dream

The following dream is an example of how free association can help. All that remained in Ann's memory in the morning was that she had received a blow on her neck. Beginning with a literal interpretation, it had to be asked if she did have a real pain in her neck or had suffered any injury recently. On its own, this sign meant little and offered no further clues.

Through free association of ideas, Ann discovered she had no physical pain whatsoever, nor did she know anyone else who had hurt their neck. Her thoughts led her to the previous day when she met up with a friend from the past. Memories from twenty years ago flooded back and among these were incidents which, when remembered, still irritated her intensely. Returning again to the question of her neck, the message struck her instantly. The friend from the past had been, and still was, metaphorically speaking, a pain the neck.

Emotional Triggers

Beneath the surface of a dream there may also lie emotional triggers. These can be the instigators of dreams. When our unconscious registers traumatic incidents, they usually bury themselves in the 'cellar' of the mind. Down there, they become disguised and distorted so that they are more palatable at the conscious, surface level. Emotional triggers are what Freud called 'day residues'. When awake we engage in many different non-physical struggles — conscience, greed, aggression, likes, dislikes and many more feelings. The incidents precipitating these feelings are insignificant compared with the emotional trauma they leave in their wake, and it is these, lying downstairs in our dreaming mind, that act as instigators of dreams.

The more disturbing an emotional incident is, the more elusive and difficult it is to recognise in a conscious way, but once recognised, it becomes surprisingly evident. It is the realisation that we have suppressed or disguised something in this way that gives us a glimpse of our defences and the need for psychological self-preservation.

None of us is without emotionally charged life experiences, therefore no dream is without at least some emotionally charged element. When we unconsciously disguise one of these elements, we bring our entire life history and resources to bear on it. The way to decode this is to try to associate the apparent meaningless symbol with the first thing that comes into our head, and progress from there.

Problem Solving

Those who sleep for eight hours a day, and hence dream more, have been found to be more creative and better able to deal with life's problems than those who are deprived in this way. People awoken by alarm clocks are constantly being denied their full quota of sleep and dreams, and this deprivation manifests during waking hours as bad moods, sluggish responses and generally not being able to cope and give of their best at work. Sleep and dreaming are, therefore, vital activities which we need to support us when we are awake and thinking logically.

Written into every dream is a message, but in addition to this, advice and solutions are often given. Apart from literal messages which we can take at face value, there are those with their messages just below the surface. To discover these we have to follow the clues in a practical way and, as with the association of ideas, arrive at surprising but applicable conclusions and even remedies.

The dreamer who had suffered from persistent night fevers for years, despite medication from several doctors, was told in his dream to ask his doctor for a 'tonic'. On waking, he thought this an unlikely cure but nevertheless followed its advice so decided to go to his doctor and ask for this. On his way there, he passed an off-licence and in the window was a display of different tonic waters.

Almost on impulse, he went in and bought a dozen bottles, went home and drank a bottle of this each day. After a few days he noticed he had not had a fever during the night, so he continued taking the rest of the tonic water.

How did his dreaming mind know that tonic water contained quinine, a well-known remedy for fevers due to parasitic infection? Somewhere, either in a consciously forgotten memory or through an unconscious link with the collective unconscious, this information surfaced in a dream. But, as with all dreams, it needed the conscious self to carry out the message offered in this way.

Inventive Dreams

Inventive people are renowned for sleeping well into the day. It is said that Leonardo da Vinci, the world's greatest inventor ever, slept almost as long as he was awake. Throughout history there are examples of discoveries revealed in dreams but these unique revelations do not simply come out of the blue to any dreamer. They arrive as counterparts to conscious efforts carried out during waking hours, as in the case of Professor von Kekule, on page 34.

Other problems have been solved during sleep only by following a complex chain of reasoning beginning with events far removed from both the cause and the solution. An anagram — SCNACEDELIHSKR — was set for a sleeping subject, producing a dream about Dempsey and Makepeace, two television personalities. One of them reminded the dreamer of a friend she had called Carol. Carol reminded her of *A Christmas Carol* which led her to its author, CHARLES DICKENS, the answer to the anagram.

In a less academic but, nonetheless, profound exercise, the dreamer who was on the point of throwing her knitting away because she could not understand the complicated pattern it involved, found that by dreaming about it from sheer frustration and desperation, she was able to follow the instructions without the slightest difficulty next day, even though she did not remember details of the dream.

The Computer Brain

Brains have been compared with radio, television and now computers. In some ways this is an excellent analogy, for not only do brains store information, they sort it all out when off-line, or asleep, as well. Sometimes we can leave our brains to their own devices and receive helpful or warning dreams spontaneously, but at other times we have consciously to programme it, like a computer, and ask for help.

We know that images in dreams are crucial to our understanding of those dreams, but the reasoning used to transform them from abstract scenes to practical solutions is rarely logical or linear. A very different pattern of thought and approach, linked not only with intelligence but with intuition, instinct and creativity, has to be employed. As a form of oblique thinking, this technique can be applied to certain everyday situations as well as dreams. Not surprisingly, it brings about remarkable conclusions that could never have been dreamed up logically.

Punning Dreams

Both Freud and Jung observed that dreams often contain puns. Some nations use puns as part of their humour more than others so it follows that dreamers from those countries tend to use puns in their dreams. Jokes are often based on these because they represent a simple but effective way of bringing together ideas that are normally considered to be unrelated. This is the basis of all originality and lateral thinking.

There are verbal puns where one word represents another with similar pronunciation but different spelling. For example, the woman who dreamed she was dressed in a long gilt dress soon realised this represented feelings of guilt that she would not allow to come to the surface.

Some pun dreams are based on visual puns where a scene

expresses an idea involving a different sense for the same word. An example of this is the woman who had no interest whatsoever in cricket yet dreamed of a game being played in her back garden. Relating this to her behaviour over a personal matter, she decided her attitude was 'not cricket'.

There are also puns based on proper names. A baker may represent a Mr Baker whom the dreamer knows or, conversely, a dream about a garden could be hinting at someone with the name of Gardner.

Colours and Dreams

Tradition says that we use colours in our dreams to highlight certain things in our life. Bright, clear colours indicate positive aspects and trends whereas dull, drab colours have negative associations. Although personal likes and dislikes for particular colours obviously affect the message, white, black, and each of the seven colours nevertheless have their own collective meaning:

WHITE Purity, illumination, honesty, innocence and relief from pressures are portrayed. But, depending on the circumstances in the dream, white may indicate a colourless existence.

BLACK An accepted colour denoting the end of a phase, death, total negation or hidden aspects of life. It indicates shades of mourning and death, gloom and depression. Alternatively, night, passiveness, receptivity and motherliness are offered.

RED A colour denoting physical energy and strength. Depending on the circumstances in the dream it can mean either renewed vigour, or it can warn against rage and anger, as in the case of the red rag to a bull syndrome.

ORANGE Social activities and relationships are under scrutiny when this colour is dominant. It also has the power to change a dismal atmosphere into one of cheerfulness, and matters of a trivial nature are also indicated.

YELLOW The need for clear thinking and intellectual reflection is represented in this light. The message is: 'Think with the head, not with the heart.' On the negative side, it indicates cowardice.

GREEN In the not too distant past all classrooms and hospitals were painted green. This was because green has a very calming, relaxing effect, so when it appears in a dream, it is telling the dreamer to take time off and rest more. Green in natural surroundings will bring relaxing moments, so a visit to the country would be helpful. This colour can also suggest envy and jealousy.

BLUE Blue, and sky blue in particular, means the dreamer is protected from whatever it is that may be threatening him or her. Confidence and renewed hopes are restored as a result. On the negative side, look for any cold, calculating facts which may bring about a blue mood.

INDIGO Instinct and intuition are stirring with this mysterious colour, bringing a realisation that the physical world is not the only world. It also urges: 'Think with the head, not with the heart'.

VIOLET This colour is nearest to heaven, denoting spiritual matters, altruistic feelings and all things of other worldliness.

BROWN Devotion to duty is indicated, but to some, a depressing feeling fills the air.

GOLD Sunshine and happiness are indicated.

CHAPTER EIGHT

THE DICTIONARY OF SIGNS AND SYMBOLS

We create our dreams from our own dream language, which is a combination of collective symbolism and our own. A dream dictionary can give the traditional symbolic meanings common to all but it cannot reveal the meaning of those signs which, from past experience, have unique, personal associations.

When interpreting your dreams you must, therefore, learn your own inner language as well as understanding traditional meanings found in collective symbolism and metaphor. It helps if you think of each dream as an original work of art, for that is what it is. And, like all paintings, some will be literal scenes while others project abstract impressions which, at first glance, seem to be totally meaningless. These will be the symbolic dreams.

When you relate collective and personal meanings to your own circumstances, you will soon know the reason for a dream and understand its message. Remember, too, that the skilful dream interpreter is the person who has the ability to recognise resemblances and look-alike situations in the form of analogies, metaphors and comparisons. In the form of parables, these can have meanings far more powerful than any literal image or words.

A

Abandoned To feel alone and forsaken is self-explicit. It also contains the message urging self-motivation and not self-pity.

Abattoir This is a warning sign. A life-threatening situation or domination looms nearer so beware of the inevitable.

Abbess An idealistic woman.

Abbey The mansion of the soul, representing the dreamer as a whole. High ideals of a spiritual nature, and protection from the real world.

Abbot A man with high ideals.

Abduction To be taken or removed from a place against your will warns of gross interference with personal liberty.

Abdomen This generally means vulnerability concerning a situation that cannot be 'stomached'. A large abdomen means 'great expectations', a small abdomen warns of lean times.

Abortion A warning that plans may abort. It also means regrets over hasty decisions. Beware, too, of a miscarriage of justice.

Abroad Travel is likely which may or may not solve a problem. A 'foreign' experience could occur.

Abundance Multiplicity or plenty is always a good sign but can be understood only when related to personal circumstances.

Abyss This reveals a down-in-the dumps situation. Things cannot get worse, only better. A very testing time is to be expected.

Accident Take this as a literal warning telling you to take extra care in a related situation or circumstances. Symbolically, it means you are punishing yourself. If the accident happened to someone else, it shows you have aggressive feelings for that person.

Accounts This shows you are 'balancing the books'. Credits and deficits are being assessed. It could warn of over-spending not only money but personal energy as well.

Ace This sign offers encouragement for success. A prize or win literally or metaphorically.

Ace of Clubs Financial security ahead.

Ace of Diamonds New ventures, especially careers and business, will bring rewards.

Ace of Hearts Romance and friendships will flourish.

Ace of Spades This warns of a considerable obstacle ahead.

Acorn Great potential for the future lies ahead. Look for family associations.

Acrobat Difficulties can be overcome if you tackle them in a roundabout way, using ingenuity.

Actor and/or Actress Beware of those around you who are false and acting out an unnatural role.

Adam and Eve Partnerships are under scrutiny. Questions of heritage and inheritances will arise.

Adultery This reflects guilty feelings, not only concerning sexual relationships. Look, too, for corruption around you.

Aeroplane High flying aims and ambitions are being viewed. If the plane crashes it means you must bring ideals down to earth. If it lands safely, you can expect success.

Africa This continent represents the dreamer's unknown potential and offers a future more expansive and exciting than the past.

Afternoon A specified time in a dream relates to time left to accomplish something. It also indicates middle-age.

Air To be aware of air in a dream means freedom at last. It also offers inspirational ideas which solve problems.

Aisle To be walking down an aisle means there is little choice in life but to go on. As a pun, it relates to an isle, an island, which in turn indicates possible isolation.

Alarm The feeling of alarm or hearing an alarm bell ringing is a definite warning sign relating to something known only to the dreamer.

Albatross This bird symbolises a good omen for the future.

Alligator This creature is a warning sign so beware of extreme opposition or being 'swallowed' into a collective situation that robs you of personal identity.

Almonds Depending on other circumstances in the dream, and on personal circumstances, this nut warns of bitterness. It also has bitter-sweet content with special healing associations.

Altar Undoubtedly self-sacrifice is indicated. Beware of becoming a martyr rather than a willing victim or participant.

Ambassador To dream of an ambassador emphasises the necessity to present oneself in a positive, diplomatic way.

Amber This resinous, semi-precious stone is easily charged with electricity. Unconsciously, this fact is known so when seen in a dream it relates to personal attraction and physical energy.

America Travel is indicated, not necessarily to America. It also suggests duality and parallel events.

Amethyst This stone brings peace of mind.

Ammunition Beware of dangerous tongues, verbal ambushes and attacks. Do not fire the bullets made by others — in other words do not pass on negative information.

Amulet This charm is a sign of protection so be ever watchful for attack, both physical and emotional.

Anagram Scrambled letters warn of hidden meanings.

Ancestors To dream of ancestors tells of inherited characteristics — some good, some bad.

Anchor Beware of wandering from the point. Strong attachments to a person or a place are indicated.

Angel An angel in a dream is a dream messenger.

Anima This is the Jungian term for the feminine, compassionate side of man's nature. As an inner image, it is a composite of all the females the dreamer has known, beginning with his mother. It is 'the woman of his dreams'.

Animals Animals, generally, symbolise the basic nature of humanity, especially the physical and psychological craving for sex and food. They may be saying the dreamer is a pig, boar or an outright beast.

Animus This is the Jungian term for the male, practical side of a woman's nature. As with the anima, all men known to the dreamer help to form this image. It is 'the man of her dreams'.

Anvil The forging of bonds, especially friendships, are under the hammer of consideration. Physical strength is on the increase.

Ape To see this creature in a dream, unless associated with a recent visit to the zoo, indicates regression in one form or another.

Apples This fruit offers healing and good health. It also signifies a sexual appetite.

Apricots Good health and good fortune are on the way.

Aquamarine Eternal youth and lasting friendship are signified by this stone.

Arch Unification lies ahead. Promotion and realisation of hopes, aims and ambitions can be relied upon.

Archer An archer in a dream determines the way and the aim. He may also signify a person born under the sign of Sagittarius.

Ark To see an image of the ark in a dream urges careful planning and protection, especially where family matters are concerned.

Arm An arm symbolises physical effort.

Army Others may be for you or against you so beware of opposition or attack.

Arrow To see an arrow obviously indicates direction in life. It also means you should set your sights on a future goal and aim for this. Hearts may be pierced with this so relationships and romance could be in the air.

Artist This character is the creative person within.

Ascending Going up stairs or ascending in an elevator means hopes are rising. Obstacles will be overcome and a clearer, more expansive vision helps you understand problems objectively.

Ashes These represent past memories. Look for a 'sackcloth and ashes' scene metaphorically. Beware of the martyr syndrome.

Asia This continent, personal and cultural associations apart, represents undiscovered characteristics in oneself and others. Mystery and surprises are ahead.

Asparagus Forging ahead is indicated, symbolised by the spearhead of this vegetable. Social success is particularly likely.

Ass This maligned animal represents the fool in society — and in dreams. As a warning sign, beware of becoming this. Furthermore, do not carry other people's burdens because they will not thank you.

Assassin To see a killer in your dream is a serious warning. You may wish to annihilate an aspect of your own personality or metaphorically want to destroy or kill a relationship.

Astronaut Astronauts are recent dream characters personifying adventure and youthful masculine pursuits. Beware of immaturity.

Atoms These symbolise the underlying pattern and structure of a particular situation or problem. Beware of paying too much attention to detail thus missing the main object.

Attack To be attacked in your dream is a definite warning, so protect yourself from both physical harm and psychological intrusion.

Attic This is the top room in the Mansion of the Soul, symbolising high ideals and aspiring hopes for the future. Spiritual beliefs, intuition, instincts, intellect and conscience are all stored up here.

Auction Beware of bartering and competition as well as swift disposal of assets and friends.

Aunt This is a supportive feminine influence which gives confidence to the dreamer.

Audience To be in front of an audience shows you need to be seen and heard. Make sure others pay more attention to you but also make sure you play your part well.

Australia Personal association apart, this continent represents a new beginning full of better opportunities. Forget the past and look forward to the future.

Automobile This vehicle represents the dreamer and his or her driving force within. To be driving an automobile shows you are in control of your destiny but much depends on the speed, the road and the hazards in the way. Associate the scene with real life events and the message will become clear.

Autumn Time is running out so make the most of today. There is much to reap from the past so make the most of this too.

Avalanche This offers a strong warning concerning a sweeping statement or situation that makes you a victim of circumstances.

Aviator In a woman's dream the high-flyer is her animus, the man of her dreams. In a man's dream he symbolises the hero.

B

Baboon Baboons represent basic, human tendencies which are generally seen as regressive behaviour. To see one in your dream may be self-reflection, or the image of someone else.

Baby Unless you are anticipating having a baby, a baby symbolises the dreamer's brainchild. It is the new, unique idea full of future potential. Someone else's baby warns of taking on other people's troubles but if it grows quickly it means success will soon be yours.

Bachelor Married men often dream of being this, thus indicating their desire for freedom. When a woman dreams of a bachelor it reflects her search for the 'ideal man'.

Back When only the back of a person is seen in a dream it warns you not to jump to conclusions. It also means you are excluded from something that is going on behind your back.

Badger This animal represents an undercover worker reaping little reward. It also signifies a fear of going bald.

Bag As a play on words a 'bag' stands for a particular woman. It also represents heavy commitments.

Bagpipes These vibes excite basic feelings and incite physical activity such as dancing and fighting.

Baker A good sign indicating that all will turn out right in the end.

Balcony An extended, elevated view of one's affairs is necessary. For lovers, there is a warning of a fond adieu.

Baldness To see a bald-headed man in your dream tells you to keep calm, or to 'keep your hair on', as the saying goes.

Ball A ball symbolises the world. It also represents life; the game of life. A golden ball, as in fairy tales, means greater understanding and the gift of wisdom.

Ballet Dancing in dreams heralds romance. Ballet dancing shows the need for calculated moves in a balanced way. To see a ballet performed on a stage means the dreamer will have an opportunity to enjoy the finer things in life.

Balloons To see these in your dreams tells you to make light of certain problems and try to rise above them. To ride in a balloon basket means you will be in an excellent position to make clear, far-seeing decisions.

Banana Freudians may see this as a phallic symbol. This fruit, however, traditionally represents protracted, long-drawn-out business or emotional affairs.

Bandage As a literal sign, take a bandage as a warning against physical injury. Symbolically it indicates the necessity for greater protection on all levels.

Bandits When these appear in your dream beware of those around you who think they are above and beyond the law.

Bank A bank represents a deposit place for treasured memories which provide a wealth of personal experience.

Bankruptcy This warns of depleted resources. Reserves, relating not only to money but to energy, have not built up sufficiently to protect against hard times.

Banjo This musical instrument is associated with a country and western lifestyle. Beware of recklessness in yourself or others. Anatomically, it symbolises the neck and body.

Bantam A bantam denotes a small but spirited person. It also represents an idea which is not fully fledged so it can never become reality. Replanning is necessary.

Baptism Baptism is a universally ancient ceremony of initiation symbolising rebirth and the washing away of past negativity. It also denotes the end of a phase and the beginning of a new, more hopeful one.

Barber If someone cuts your hair beware of a loss of energy, strength or determination. Traditionally, it relates to radical measures or surgery.

Barefoot To walk barefoot shows the need to be in closer contact with earthly, basic facts. To do this also warns of treading on dangerous ground.

Barge As a pun, to see a barge in your dream warns you not to 'barge' in where you are not wanted. Symbolically, it means your life compares with sailing on still waters. This could mean boredom.

Bark To be aware of bark on a tree means you can proceed with confidence in the knowledge that you are well protected. If the bark is damaged it warns of vulnerability.

Barking Barking dogs are a distinct warning that danger, in one form or another, is approaching.

Barley This grain represents health and strength as well as signifying potential expansion and a good harvest in the future.

Barn As a building a barn represents an aspect of the Mansion of the Soul. It is the place where treasured memories are stored, in readiness to be recalled in times of need.

Barometer Beware of mood swings and changes of character which upset the balance.

Barrier To see any barrier in a dream is self-explicit. It clearly means an obstacle lies ahead which has to be recognised and overcome, either by acceptance or by getting round it.

Basement This part of a house symbolises the deepest level in the Mansion of the Soul. Down here you store all your unconscious desires and fears.

Basket A basket is a vessel carrying sustenance and benevolence. It tells of good fortune, plenty and friendship in the future. Much depends on what and how much is in the basket.

Bat If you are afraid of bats then to you they symbolise frightening attacks from unknown sources. If, on the other hand, you find these creatures interesting, then in a dream they are telling you to use your sense of direction and see those things which have so far remained hidden from you.

Bath To be having a bath in a dream means you need to wash away past indiscretions and fears and begin anew.

Battle A battle scene indicates trouble so be ready for encounters where you may well be out-numbered.

Bayonet A very sharp, pointed emotional or verbal attack is likely. This can be avoided if you are vigilant.

Bazaar Life could become confused when a bazaar appears in your dream. Surprises, both good and bad, come to light.

Beads A chain of social events can be expected. If the beads are broken, be warned of broken promises.

Bear Traditionally, and in the collective unconscious, a bear represents an overpowering force of a feminine nature. It also symbolises the USSR.

Beard As a strong sign of masculinity the message behind a beard is one of strength and conviction. Beware, however, of outer appearances which disguise inner, less charitable characteristics.

Beasts So-called bestial instincts are represented by beasts of burden. Heraldic or mythological beasts symbolise archetypal forces and principles.

Beaten To be beaten at a game in your dreams warns of others getting the better of you.

Beaver To see a beaver in your dreams means you will reap considerable rewards, but first you will have to work like the proverbial creature.

Beef Raw flesh indicates that the sensual and basic side of life is under consideration. A hanging carcass represents hopelessness and is sometimes related to an illness.

Beehive Much activity can be expected and generally a beehive is a sign of prosperity through personal and communal effort. A hive devoid of bees warns of financial problems.

Bees A lone bee is the ancient symbol of royalty indicating an inheritance. To see a swarm of bees is also a fortunate sign but if you are stung by a bee in your dream, it warns you of a unwarranted, unexpected attack.

Beetles As insects, beetles represent small but persistent annoyances. A scarab or dung beetle symbolises inner potential yet to be realised.

Beetroot To see this root in your dream suggests feelings of guilt and shyness. This image no doubt arises from the saying 'blushing as red as a beetroot'.

Beggar When this figure appears in your dream it usually means you are looking at a down-and-out aspect of yourself. Consider personal needs and try to attain them without enlisting help from others.

Beheaded Beware of 'losing your head'. Beheading is a ritual symbolising a separation of the head from the heart, intelligence from intuition, so remember to keep the balance.

Bells Hearing a bell ring is a reminder. A peal of bells heralds good news. Often the noise from the telephone or the ringing of the front doorbell is incorporated into a dream where it is put into some context.

Belt Metaphorically, this object is generally tightened in times of need so take a belt as a sign telling you to be thrifty and careful, especially where money is concerned.

Bereavement Unless this feeling can be related to a real event, it is telling you that you will have regrets unless you make amends before it is too late.

Berry Fruit of this nature symbolises reward from past labour. As a pun it means you should 'bury the past' and let bygones be bygones.

Bet Betting in a dream tells you to take a chance by remembering the saying 'nothing ventured, nothing gained'.

Bewitched If you feel someone is bewitching you beware of the fact that you are falling under someone's domination. Do not be taken in with what others say or do — be true to yourself.

Bible To see a bible in your dreams means you are seeking the truth, not necessarily religious truth but an understanding of a basic question.

Bicycle Riding a bicycle shows you are making much progress along your destinational path in life, entirely through your own physical effort. You are certainly travelling in the right direction, but must expect there to be uphill struggles from time to time.

Binoculars This indicates your need to see into the future or, at least, to look ahead carefully. On a cautious note they warn you not to pry too much into the personal affairs of others.

Birds Birds are common symbols in dreams indicating personal high-flying aims and ambitions of an idealistic nature. A flight of birds warns against flights of fancy, whereas a caged bird reflects caged-in feelings, so free yourself from limitations which may be self-imposed. A bird may also symbolise the spirit of a person, dead or alive.

Birth Giving birth in a dream symbolises the birth of a new idea. To see a birth means re-birth, a new beginning for the dreamer and generally birth means there is great hope for the future.

Birthday To dream of your birthday tells you to count your blessings and also to remind yourself that it is later than you think.

Biscuits Sweet memories from the past have been conjured up. A prize may be in the offing.

Bishop This figure represents a particular characteristic of the dreamer or that of a respected person.

Black Black is associated with death, winter, and the end of a phase. Depending on personal feelings and circumstances it can also denote Mother Earth and passiveness.

Blackberries In tradition, blackberries symbolise setbacks. This reputation probably arose from the superstition that they provided food for the devil.

Blackbirds These birds bring warnings concerning funereal and territorial rights. They also represent domineering characteristics.

Blacksmith As a collective sign a blacksmith means better times are ahead. It also indicates that physical effort will provide more reward than mental consideration.

Blanket Beware of problems arising from unseen circumstances. Look for hidden, undercover meanings.

Blind To be unable to see clearly indicates that the truth is hidden from you.

Blood Blood in a dream symbolises the life force and physical energy. It also means anger in the form of hot-blooded tempers. To lose blood warns of a loss of virility and strength.

Blossom Happiness, contentment and youthful pursuits are indicated but do not expect these to last.

Blush Guilt or shyness are always indicated when a blush is seen in a dream.

Boa Constrictor As a snake, a boa represents energy, especially energy used to restrict the dreamer. Beware of a friend who interferes with your free will.

Boar As a pun, look for a boring character. In its own dream-right, this creature represents a pig-headed person or an ignoramus. Metaphorically, beware of placing 'pearls before swine'.

Boat To be on a boat indicates a destinational journey associated with emotional matters. Much depends on the circumstances and the state of the water, so the dream may indicate a rough passage ahead or that still waters run deep.

Body To see a body or torso is often a health-warning concerning something that is soon to be revealed.

Bomb This object is warning the dreamer of imminent danger. The explosion may relate to verbal abuse or a catastrophe of another nature.

Bones Hard times are predicted when bones are seen in a dream. They may also mean that there is a need to get down to the bare essentials of a particular problem.

Book A book symbolises information. If it is closed the message is that investigation into past events is desirable but if its text is visible it means you can learn from your own experiences.

Boomerang As a metaphor, a boomerang means things will come back at you, so beware of rebounding circumstances.

Boots These indicate there are new avenues to explore. If the boots appear to be old, pay more attention to personal matters.

Bouquet A reward can be expected for your efforts.

Borrow If you try to borrow from another in your dream, beware of dwindling resources. If, however, someone tries to borrow from you, it means you are a source of help and support.

Bow A bow minus arrows tells you that you must aim for the future without delay.

Box Depending on the nature of the box, it may represent a treasure chest, in which case you can expect a surprise, or it may signify a coffin, so beware of a deathwish in the air.

Boy A boy in a man's dream symbolises the dreamer as he thinks he is, or as he would like to be. In a woman's dream, a boy is either her son or the youthful aspect of her animus.

Bracelet Bracelets, like rings, symbolise unions and reunions. If it is broken, it warns of damaged friendships and relationships.

Brake A brake indicates the necessity to slow down and take life a little easier.

Brambles Hindrances and minor difficulties may be encountered which hold back progress and the achievement of certain aims.

Branches Branches of a tree represent branches or members of the family.

Brass To see brass objects in a dream warns of false deals. Money matters are represented by this metal.

Bread Bread symbolises food for thought as well as the physical body. To share bread with another person means rewards will be reaped soon for this is akin to 'casting your bread upon the water'.

Break To break anything in a dream warns of finality. If there are several fragments it means you should metaphorically pick up the pieces and start again.

Breath If you are aware of your breath or breathing in a dream it indicates a need for healing, the receiving of the breath of life.

Breeze Expect winds of change to bring about refreshing alterations in your life.

Bricks Bricks represent the essential parts of a problem, situation or circumstance. Laying bricks warns against empire-building and acquiring more than you can manage.

Bride She may be the dreamer's image of herself. The bride also symbolises femininity and the receptive counterpart of an individual.

Bridge A bridge in a dream represents the link between two stages, situations, choices, solutions or problems. To be on a bridge means a decision must be reached soon, so choose which way to go in life.

Brook A brook symbolises free and easy times. Emotions are easily swayed.

Broom Much depends on surrounding circumstances but a broom in a dream, as in everyday metaphorical language, indicates sweeping changes are to be made.

Brother When the dreamer is a man, his brother may represent rivalry or brotherly love towards someone, not necessarily his brother. In a woman's dream, her brother represents platonic friendship with a man other than her brother.

Brown This colour often sets the backcloth for a dream, as in a 'brown study'. To some, it suggests depression but to others brown is a warm, natural colour relating to Mother Earth and basic things in life.

Buildings If the dreamer is involved in the construction or purchase of buildings, to see one in their dream may be a literal reference to this. Symbolically, a building represents the dreamer as a whole, the Mansion of the Soul, yet at the same time highlighting a particular characteristic. A factory, for example, points to industrious ability whereas a church indicates beliefs and high ideals.

Bull A bull represents someone who is strong and down-to-earth. If the animal appears angry beware of uncontrolled tempers and angry behaviour. Alternatively, it may symbolise a Taurean.

Bulldog This dog symbolises the archetypal British character. Individually, it relates to protection and the possible need to defend oneself.

Burglar A burglar is always a warning sign both literally and symbolically. This character represents intrusion into the dreamer's life in one form or another, so take extra care on all levels.

Burning To smell burning is a distinct warning so be careful with matches and cigarettes. Metaphorically, look for smouldering situations beneath the surface.

Bus To travel on a bus shows the dreamer's destiny is shared with others and in many ways he or she has to take a back seat. To be waiting for a bus means all opportunities should be taken as soon as they come along.

Butcher Beware of someone who will metaphorically slaughter and sacrifice other people for their own ends.

Butter The future will be far richer and easier than the past.

Butterfly To see a butterfly in a dream symbolises the dreamer's inner self — the psyche.

C

Cabbage This vegetable warns of a vegetating, time-wasting existence. It also warns of a dull outlook.

Cage A cage clearly represents restrictions and inhibitions which may be self-imposed or not, as the case may be.

Cake Sweet but short-lived moments are represented by cakes. They also warn of over-indulgence and too much of the good things in life.

Calendar A calendar serves as a reminder, usually indicating that time is running out.

Calf Young love is indicated when a calf appears in a dream but if it is fat, beware of being sacrificed for another's interest and betterment.

Camel Since these animals are beasts of burden beware of carrying too many problems on your back, especially those of others.

Camera A camera means personal secrets should be well guarded.

Canal The collective unconscious invariably sees canals as relating to childbirth and the delivery of a baby.

Canary A singing canary promises romantic moments in the near future. If the bird is not singing, it is a warning that danger is in the air.

Cancer To dream of this shows a fear of illness. On a symbolic level it relates to someone born under the zodiacal sign of Cancer.

Candle A lighted candle indicates strength of purpose and hope for the future. An unlit candle warns of wasted opportunity, deprivation and disappointment.

Cannibal To see cannibals symbolises self-destruction in one form or another. It also warns of total domination and possession either of the dreamer or by the dreamer.

Canoe A canoe, like a ship, represents the dreamer's destinational journey over life's calm or troubled waters. If alone in a canoe, self-sufficiency and self-reliance are called for.

Canyon A rift or divided opinion will soon appear on the horizon.

Captain Considerable responsibility will be expected but with this goes a rise in status.

Car See automobile.

Cards Playing cards denote the game of life, with each suit representing one of its four aspects. Hearts relate to love and friendships; Diamonds relate to business affairs, careers and aims; Clubs relate to financial matters and rich rewards reaped from good deeds; and Spades relate to inevitable obstacles.

Carnation This flower is a sign of reincarnation, renewed life, rebirth and birth. A flowering of the personality may also be expected.

Carols An excellent year ahead can confidently be expected.

Carpet A complicated design on a carpet represents the intricacies of life's rich pattern. If the carpet is of an over-all colour beware of 'being on the carpet'.

Carrots The Freudian significance cannot be ignored but this vegetable also has to be seen as an inducement, temptation or bribe.

Castle This stronghold is a version of the Mansion of the Soul showing resolute aims and steadfastness.

Castration To dream of castration symbolically warns of loss of respect and status, as well as a fear of unmanliness.

Cat If the dreamer is fond of cats, a cat symbolises the feminine, intuitive side of their nature, but if they dislike them, it represents female cattiness and spite. A black cat is always a good, positive sign for the future.

Catastrophe Whether an earthquake or other upheaval, such an event warns of trouble ahead. It may be of a physical nature or in the form of an emotional catastrophe.

Caterpillar Seeing one of these warns of immediate difficulties, but later on, considerable changes bring out-of-the-ordinary reward.

Cathedral This edifice symbolises the dreamer's high ideals and spiritual beliefs.

Cattle A herd of cattle represents the majority, not the individual, so beware of losing personal identity.

Cave A cave symbolises the inner realm, the unconscious. It also represents a return to pre-natal days and ancestral inheritance. A mythological cave, where a dragon guards the entrance, means hidden treasure lies within but access to this is difficult.

Cedar Tree Trees symbolise family matters. A cedar tree has particular associations with Celtic myth and ancestral Celtic roots.

Ceiling A ceiling in a dream means ambitions and aims have not yet been attained because it is difficult to go beyond a certain point. 'A ceiling has been reached', so changes are necessary before the breakthrough can occur.

Cell To be imprisoned in a cell warns of certain restrictions either self-imposed or circumstantial. It may also represent a single idea or isolated hope for the future.

Cellar As the basement of the Mansion of the Soul, dark thoughts and memories are often found here. Hidden fears, basic instincts and strong feelings also reside but these are beginning to reveal themselves.

Cemetery A graveyard is often associated in dreams with thoughts of departed relatives, friends and the past, which is also dead. Depression and hopelessness is also signified.

Centre When a central point is seen in a dream it means the innermost self is being revealed. To be in the centre of a town or village indicates that you are very near to your aim or goal in life.

Chains Invisible yet strong links bind the dreamer to someone or something.

Chair An empty chair signifies a vacancy. Depending on personal circumstances, this can be seen as a promotional sign or as a sad loss.

Chalice This vessel offers the waters of life which bring healing for body, mind and spirit.

Chameleon Beware of someone who disguises their true nature. Additionally, a certain situation may not be what it seems.

Chapel Chapels symbolise the holy or spiritual part of the dreamer's Mansion of the Soul. It houses their special beliefs.

Chase To be chased by an unknown person or creature shows there is a conflict within the dreamer which is pursuing them. When the pursuer is an animal it means you are trying to escape from your own angry, basic self whom you have not consciously recognised. Running away from a difficult or frightening situation is often symbolised in this way.

Cherries This fruit warns of romantic temptations which lead to problems.

Chess This game symbolises the game of life where fate, destiny and the will of the gods play their hand.

Chest A chest, open or closed, symbolises the inner self which contains treasures in the form of personal potential.

Chicken A chicken shows that aims and ambitions exist but the dreamer cannot 'get them off the ground'. To eat the flesh of a chicken warns of cowardliness.

Child The child in a dream may be the infantile nature within the dreamer, warning of one's childish nature. It can also be a sign showing the dreamer's brain-child is growing and maturing.

Chimney An escape mechanism may be necessary. This will probably be associated with family matters since the hearth and chimney are the focal point of the home.

Chimney-Sweep As in tradition, a chimney-sweep is a sign of good fortune and a wedding.

China China, as a nation, suggests an oriental outlook.

Choke Choking in a dream is fairly common and is often due to the tongue falling back into the throat when sleeping on one's back. This feeling is then incorporated into a dream. Symbolically, it signifies a situation that metaphorically cannot be swallowed, or when sadness abounds, 'choking back the tears' becomes a dream reality.

Christ To dream of Jesus Christ means help and protection are at hand, thus faith will be restored. As an archetype He symbolises perfection, immortality and healing.

Christmas A festive time can be expected. News from afar will bring happiness and security.

Church This building signifies the dreamer's beliefs and faith. It is also a haven, a place of safety and peace within.

Cigarettes To see cigarettes or to be smoking one means you need a diversion in life and should relax more.

Cinders These indicate that past memories can be recalled but such events cannot be rekindled.

Circle A circle symbolises the innermost self surrounded by the cycle of life. It also represents the world, the universe and time.

Circus Maybe life is going in circles, so beware of boring repetition.

City A city is a collective sign relating to the outer world, including people the dreamer encounters.

Clean Cleanliness, as opposed to dirt, offers comparison between two situations. Clean clothes represent moral standards and the keeping-up of standards generally.

Climb To climb stairs, a hill or a mountain shows life is an uphill struggle but, nonetheless, progress is being made in the right direction. This action also indicates striving towards the top.

Cliff To be looking into the distance from the top of a cliff shows that the dreamer is comparatively safe at present but if care is not taken, danger could lie ahead. To be at the bottom of a cliff, looking up at it, means you are facing an obstacle of considerable proportions.

Cloak If you are wearing a cloak you know you are well protected from harm, especially from verbal attack. To see someone else wearing one tells you they are covering up something they wish to hide.

Clock Time is important to you. Is it later than you think?

Cloth Cloth symbolises the fabric of life. Patterns reflect intricate experiences woven into it, and the quality of the cloth relates to the smoothness or roughness of such experiences.

Clothes The personality and façade of the dreamer are represented by clothes in a dream. To be putting on clothes shows a change of image is to be considered. To have no clothes on means the dreamer feels prying eyes may discover their innermost secret.

Clouds The present may be clouded by a worrying episode. Conversely, they may be clearing, in which case things will surely be much brighter.

Clover To see clover growing or being picked is a most encouraging sign.

Clown To see this character in your dream warns you of making a fool of yourself.

Coal To see lumps of coal or a coalmine indicates great strength of purpose, potential energy and inner strength.

Coat This garment represents the outer façade of the personality. It may be put on for certain occasions, or may indicate the necessity of protection against cold attitudes and values.

Cobweb Cobwebs indicate that there are minor restrictions around you which can easily be swept away once they are recognised. Beware of entangling circumstances which prevent escape later.

Cock As with a chicken, limitations are indicated. In the Freudian sense, beware of lustful intentions.

Coffin The main message of a coffin is that there is no escape from a particular situation. To see yourself lying in one means you have reached the final phase of something in life and should begin on the next round. Metaphorically, a coffin says 'I wish I were dead' — a statement not to be confused with a deathwish.

Coins Financial improvement is bound to happen soon but coins also signify wealth of opportunity, wealth of understanding and a wealth of happiness; all assets in the bank of human experience.

Cold To feel cold points out feelings of neglect, emotional frigidity and generally being left out in the cold. It also suggests a freezing fear and lack of warmth.

Collision Arguments and head-on social and verbal encounters are to be avoided.

Colours The intensity of colour sets the backcloth for a dream. Dullness indicates depression and a negative setting, whereas brightness shows that an improvement of a situation can be expected. The dreamer's mood or state of mind is also reflected. Dreams in black and white are thought to have been in colour originally, but if this does not contribute to the dream's message, it fades from memory. Each colour symbolises an energy or principle in life. (See Chapter 7, pages 76–7, for a full explanation of the meaning of each colour.)

Comet To see this portent in a dream warns that problems are on the way.

Computer A computer represents logical thinking and computer-like reasoning.

Confetti Apart from any association with a recent or forthcoming wedding, confetti means social success.

Cooking To be cooking in your dream means you are 'cooking something up', so try not to be too devious.

Corn Corn, when it is plentiful in a dream, indicates prosperous times ahead.

Corpse To see a corpse metaphorically suggests a lifeless sort of person, but when the corpse is yourself, it means an aspect of yourself needs revitalising. A new beginning is called for.

Corridor Corridors and narrow passageways represent connections between two sets of circumstances or situations. There is no other way but to go ahead.

Cot An empty cot symbolises unfulfilled hopes, but if it is occupied, it means dreams for the future will come true.

Cottage This form of the Mansion of the Soul shows a mature personality which seeks peace of mind. Retirement plans should be considered carefully.

Countries To visit countries other than your native land in your dreams warns of foreign or unusual experiences shortly.

Cousin Help will be forthcoming from a member of the family or a close friend.

Cow This animal represents a woman whom the dreamer does not like. It may also stand in for a bovine type of person.

Crab Beware of devious manoeuvring going on under your nose. Consider those born under the sign of the Crab, too.

Cripple To see a handicapped person means someone needs practical help or emotional support. It may also represent a fear of incapacitation.

Crocodile This creature is to be seen as a warning sign associated with underhand dealings and snap decisions which bring instability.

Cross The cross is an archetypal sign of Christianity as well as representing the four elements of creation and the balance of nature. It also signifies protection from harmful outer forces.

Crossroads To be at a crossroads in a dream indicates that a point in life has been reached where an important decision has to be made, concerning which direction to take.

Crow This bird often acts as a messenger for the dead. In Celtic myth a crow symbolises Bran, the spirit of Britain.

Crowd To be with a crowd urges the dreamer to become more individualistic and not to go with the herd.

Crown Success and crowning glory are indicated when a crown appears in your dream.

Crystal Spiritual illumination and healing potential are symbolised by a crystal.

Cup A cup seen in a dream symbolises a source of energy and sustenance in time of need. It symbolises one's inner strength.

Cupboard If the cupboard is closed it represents a closed, stubborn attitude of mind. It may contain the proverbial skeleton or it may be bare.

Curtain To see a curtain in your dream means there is an obstacle which prevents progress by obscuring your view of the truth. This, however, can easily be brushed aside.

D

Daffodils These flowers stir Celtic and Welsh ancestral memories. They also bring fresh hope for the future.

Dagger A dagger seen in a dream is undoubtedly a warning, so beware of treachery and that proverbial stab in the back.

Daisy This simple flower is a symbol of love, affection and kindness.

Dam An emotional outlet is needed to allow blocked-up feelings to flow freely.

Dance A dance in a dream is a prelude to love-making. Relaxation and social activities are also indicated by this.

Darkness Depression concerning unknown factors may loom up soon. You may also have feelings of being kept in the proverbial dark over something.

Daytime The present is indicated when your dream is set in daytime. A specific time of day relates to your age. Morning: youth; afternoon: maturity; evening: old age.

Date To see a specific date means that by that time, you should have accomplished that which you have in mind. To see the date of your own death is not prophetic; it urges you to make the most of every available moment so that by that date you will have something to show for all the effort you have put into life.

Daughter In a woman's dream her daughter is an image of her former self, suggesting she should adopt a more youthful approach to life. In a man's dream she is an image of his anima.

Dawn With the dawn comes renewed hope, even if it looks a little grey.

Death Death in dreams is usually metaphorical but sometimes it is prophetic. Symbolically, it represents the end of an important phase in life, so it is 'out with the old and in with the new'. It is in this sense that death in a dream can be interpreted as birth or rebirth.

Debt Someone owes someone something but this debt may not be money.

Deep Deep water, deep caves or a deep shaft represent unplumbed depths of the unconscious.

Deluge To be in a downpour of rain or flood warns of your being swamped by emotion.

Descending Whether walking down a hill, going downstairs, descending in a lift or elevator, going down a mine or pothole, it means much the same. By applying the event to personal circumstances it can reveal that a descent is necessary in order to establish a firm footing. A temporary lowering of standards may be indicated. Delving into the unconscious where past memories are buried could solve a problem.

Desert This arid place warns of desolation and loneliness but time spent here can be turned to your advantage: find the real you.

Devil The Devil, when he appears in dreams, is a distinct warning. He personifies evil forces, influences and thoughts. These may relate to the dreamer's own experiences or they may originate from without.

Diamond This jewel symbolises the many-faceted aspects of the personality. It is the self.

Dice When dice appear in a dream they warn you not to take too many chances.

Digging When digging is seen in a dream it means you are searching for an answer.

Disaster Whatever the disaster in your dream, it must be seen as a warning sign. Trouble in some shape or form is to be expected, so take evasive or protective measures as soon as possible.

Disguise Try to see through someone or a particular situation because they are not what you think they are.

Distance Seeing into the distance tells you to look ahead positively and with as much confidence as possible.

Ditch To see a ditch or dyke tells you that something has to be bridged or overcome before you can progress towards that aim or goal.

Diving Diving into water shows the dreamer plunging into their unconscious for answers, help or information.

Divorce To dream of divorce is often a fear of such a reality. Symbolically it warns of split ideals or principles. This separation may be between the dreamer's own ideals and principles or between his or her ideals and those of someone else. A bid for independence and self-reliance is called for.

Doctor This figure symbolises the self-healer within.

Dog If the dog in your dream is friendly it symbolises a friend, but if the animal is not, then beware of the dog-in-the-manger type of person or someone with a dogmatic nature.

Doll Dolls are usually objects of affection, albeit one-way attachment. Conversely, they may be seen as images of certain people whom the dreamer dislikes.

Door Above all else, doors symbolise opportunities. If the door is locked it means you should find the key. If it is open, make sure you do not miss an excellent opening leading to your aim, goal or object in life.

Dough This substance represents money. See it as a dream-pun.

Dove This bird symbolises the Holy Spirit and the individual spirit of the dreamer. It also offers personal peace and great hope for the future.

Dragon The dragon, a mythological creature, symbolises an inner fear beyond human comprehension. Archetypally, it is a force to be reckoned with.

Drama A play, film or television programme seen in your dream represents an episode from your life. It is staged in the theatre of the mind, the imagination, where future plans, hopes and fears are dramatically enacted.

Dream-Within-A-Dream To dream you are dreaming reinforces the meaning and message you wish to convey to yourself.

Drinking Metaphorically, drinking in a dream tells you to 'drink in' an atmosphere which offers wisdom and understanding.

Driving To drive a car in your dream shows you forging ahead on your destinational road through life. If someone else is driving, beware of another person mapping out your life.

Drowning To feel you are drowning warns that you are in danger of being inundated by emotions and depths of feelings. Try to rise above this tide before it engulfs you.

Drugs To be aware of drugs in a dream warns of misleading influences and opinions.

Drum The beating of a drum tells you to pay attention to a particular situation. Listen carefully to advice even if you do not take it.

Drunk Drunkenness in a dream warns that you are intoxicated with your own ideas and exuberance.

Dusk This time of day indicates that it is later than you think.

E

Eagle Eagles symbolise high-flying ideals but beware of dominating characteristics.

Ear Listen for good news but do not pass on bad information or gossip.

Earring An unusual distinction will be bestowed upon the person seen in a dream wearing an earring.

Earth To see earth or soil in your dream symbolises principles associated with Mother Earth. Receptive ideals which form the feminine side of life are emerging.

Earthquake A disruption of some importance is to be expected. Old attitudes, values and beliefs may be overturned to prepare for a new way of life.

East Since the sun rises in the east, new hope is dawning.

Eating Partaking of a meal indicates the need for certain fulfilment and satisfaction from life generally. If eating with others, it means a sharing of ideas — food for thought — will benefit others.

Echo Hearing an echo warns of repetition or the repeating of something that should not be perpetuated.

Eclipse To see an eclipse warns you of standing in someone else's way. Conversely, be careful not to stand in the shadow of another.

Eggs The embryo of an idea which has a great part to play in the future is soon to be hatched. Easter, for example, is the time to renew pledges.

Electricity Energy, in various forms, surrounds you when it is seen in your dream, but be very careful when trying to tap this. Beware, too, of those around you who could make the sparks fly.

Elephant Someone who is large but gentle is a dependable friend. This creature also signifies motherly, reliable characteristics.

Elevator To ascend in an elevator or lift means you will rise above problems and experience a sense of achievement. To descend in an elevator or lift warns of loss of status and depression.

Elf An elf appearing in a dream represents a spirit of the elements acting as a dream messenger.

Embroidery To see embroidery warns against exaggeration.

Emerald This stone can have a psychological healing effect.

End of the World To dream of this event shows the dreamer's fear of failure and the end of a particular phase in their life.

Engine To see an engine in action represents the pumping or beating of the heart. Depending on other circumstances in the dream, the physical or emotional state of the heart and mind can be discovered.

Envelope If the envelope is sealed it means unseen dangers or problems exist, but if the envelope is open, all will be discovered.

Eruption The eruption of a volcano warns that a quarrel may develop soon.

Evil To experience the feeling of evil is a warning against someone or something that is distinctly bad.

Evening This time of day represents the latter part of life, meaning there is not much time left to do all the things planned.

Excrement This is a fortunate sign even though it is considered to be dirty; 'filthy lucre' is an example of this.

Expedition To see a party of explorers is a reminder that every avenue should be explored if an underlying cause is to be discovered.

Explosion Be prepared for explosive situations and surprises.

F

Faces Faces, usually unrecognised, often appear in early sleep. These are known as hypnotic images and are thought to be identikit faces representing types of people and their characteristics rather than individuals. Many are unpleasant characters.

Factory As a version of the Mansion of the Soul, a factory reflects the mundane, repetitive aspect of the dreamer's lifestyle. To be working in a factory in a dream shows life to be routine and boring.

Fairy A fairy is a dream messenger.

Falling The feeling of falling through space occurs in early sleep and is not a dream; it is the sensation of 'falling asleep'. To dream you are falling off a cliff or high building indicates insecurity and warns of the fear of falling from power or grace.

Family Relationship with the rest of the family is under scrutiny, so look for rivalries and deceptions.

Farm A dream-farm symbolises the domestic scene generally.

Father The dreamer's father in a dream may be the archetypal father figure, the symbol of authority and dominance. In a man's dream he is a reflection of the dreamer; in a woman's dream he is often the reflection of her animus.

Feast Seeing a feast tells you that now is the time to count your blessings and make amends.

Feathers Feathers are ancient signs indicating protection. They also represent the good things in life.

Feet Feet in dreams symbolise the path you have to tread ahead. They also warn you to keep both feet on the ground. To walk in bare feet means a good balance has been found in life.

Fence Fences represent inhibiting factors. Self-made limitations have been imposed which cause frustration.

Ferns Natural remedies and cures are represented by ferns.

Ferret Protection is needed against prying eyes and possible viciousness, when this animal appears in a dream.

Ferry For someone else to ferry you over the water warns against allowing others to do too much for you. The link between life and death is also indicated.

Field Fields or green pastures in dreams symbolise 'fields of interest' such as the arts, science, sport, etc. Better times ahead.

Figs This fruit in a dream offers enlightenment — Buddha received enlightenment whilst sitting under a fig tree, and there was also one in the Garden of Eden.

Fighting A physical struggle can mean mental conflict.

Figures Figures in a dream often represent neglected aspects of the dreamer's nature. Such shadowy forms are various unrecognised characteristics.

Film Whether the dreamer is watching a film or acting in one, it is usually an action replay of an earlier event in their life.

Film Star A film star or pop idol represents an image the dreamer admires and unconsciously mimics.

Fingers Fingers seen in a dream point a way towards a practical career or solution to a problem. Beware, too, of getting your fingers burnt if you meddle in the affairs of others.

Fire Usually powerful emotions and passions are represented and roused with this element. It is also a natural expression of burning desire, as well as hate.

Fireplace This is the hearth — the home. Warmth and emotional support are indicated.

Fish Fish symbolise the spirit of the dreamer. They also represent sustenance and the power of renewal.

Flames To see these in a dream warns of uncontrolled, flaming passions.

Flag Nationalism and patriotism are indicated when a flag is flying.

Flood Floods warn of uncontrolled emotions which inundate and swamp. To be overwhelmed by water shows certain beliefs will be swept away.

Flowers The beautiful things in life are symbolised by flowers, but each has a special message. Generally they offer the blossoming of friendship and love but if they are damaged or crushed, beware of sorrow.

Flying To experience weightlessness in a dream and rise above the ground is an experience known as astral projection. In this state some think the spirit leaves the body. Those who are able to do this can usually rise above their problems when awake, so rarely remain depressed for long.

Fog To be in a fog is self-explanatory. The truth or whatever it is you seek is hidden at present.

Font A font is a source of spiritual sustenance from whence springs energy for healing, especially self-healing.

Food Food symbolises food for thought, not sustenance for the body.

Footsteps To see or hear footsteps warns against following in other's footsteps. Lack of originality is indicated.

Foreign Land Foreign, unfamiliar events and experiences are to be expected when dreams take you to unknown territory.

Forest When forests appear in dreams, be sure you can distinguish the wood from the trees.

Forge Forges, with anvil and hammer, tell the dreamer that reliable, strong forces will restore lost confidence.

Fountain To see, and especially to drink from, a fountain is to drink the healing waters of life itself.

Fright To experience fright in a dream is always a warning sign. This has to be related to a fear known only to the dreamer.

Frog This creature offers complete transformation of character — the proverbial frog into a prince.

Funeral Seeing a funeral means the end of a particular situation is in sight. Metaphorically, it is 'their funeral'.

Furniture Furniture represents aspects of the personality as well as personal possessions.

G

Gale Better times are to be expected following the blow-up of a situation or problem. A present worry will soon blow over.

Galloping For horses to gallop through a dream indicates that the pace of life will speed up shortly.

Gambling Betting associations in dreams tell you that you can afford to take a chance.

Games Life is similar to a game. Points are won and lost and competition is between others and against oneself. Each experience is a separate game related to different aspects of life and each of these is an exercise in sportsmanship.

Garden The dream garden symbolises the dreamer's environment surrounding the Mansion of the Soul. The state of the garden reflects external conditions and any trespasses seen here are intruders into personal privacy.

Gargoyles These statue-like figures symbolise protection against negative forces, including illness.

Garlic Protection against illness is needed when garlic appears in a dream. Consider seeking medical advice if health problems exist.

Gas To smell gas in a dream is a distinct warning of an invisible danger.

Gate A gate, like a door, is an opportunity not to be missed. It also signifies the entrance to and dividing line between this and the next or other world.

Germs Germs warn of an invasion into personal rights. Health problems may also be reflected by these organisms.

Ghost To see a ghost by the bedside or in the room during sleep often signifies a visit from the dead. A ghost also represents the dreamer's own spirit.

Giant Children often dream of giants. This is not surprising when, by comparison, adults are three times as tall as them. In an adult's dream a giant symbolises the principle of strength and enormity.

Girl In a woman's dream a girl is her former self, thus representing an ever-youthful image. In a man's dream a girl he does not recognise is none other than his dream woman, his anima.

Glass A clear yet fragile situation exists when glass manifests in a dream. To break a glass warns that ideals may be shattered but a more realistic outlook will replace this.

Gloves Metaphorically, gloves in your dream mean that a particular situation needs very careful handling. To be aware of wearing gloves shows the dreamer is averse to something and wishes to distance him or herself from this. They do not wish to 'dirty their hands'.

Gnome Gnomes are spirits of nature belonging to the earth kingdom. They act as guardians of the home and personal property.

God To see God, or the Hand of God, in a dream reflects the dreamer's concept of God. It may also be a call for divine help and protection.

Gods and Goddesses Gods and goddesses personify archetypal forces and principles encountered in everyday life.

Gold When gold manifests in a dream, it symbolises a precious memory of great value.

Golf To play golf in a dream is a reflection of life, emphasising that it is single-handed experience with handicaps and few prizes.

Gorilla This animal may be mirroring the gross image of someone whom the dreamer dislikes or sees as uncivilised.

Grain Grain symbolises rewards which will be reaped from life's rich harvest.

Grass Green grass in dreams is an excellent sign of fresh pastures but parched, brown grass shows the dreamer will have to work very hard to make ends meet.

Grave A grave symbolises the past which should remain buried. To see one's own grave warns the dreamer that they should begin anew.

Gravestone This means the dreamer should analyse his or her own motives, as if writing an obituary. 'See yourself as others see you' is the message.

Great Mother This goddess appearing in a dream represents the earth, archetypally. She is the feminine principle within individuals and in nature too.

Guest An unknown guest in a dream symbolises unrecognised potential, either in oneself or in others.

Gypsy To see a gypsy or a gypsy camp, especially when smoke arises from this, warns of departure in one form or another.

H

Haemorrhage To lose blood is a warning concerning loss of, or the draining away of energy, strength and vitality.

Hair Depending on the state and type of hair, virility and attractiveness to the opposite sex can be assessed.

Half Half of anything in a dream denotes that the dreamer is halfway towards accomplishing something.

Hand If a hand appears from above it symbolises the helping Hand of God but even if the hand is not recognised as this, the message is that 'help is at hand'.

Handbag In a dream this bag represents personal identity so to lose it means the dreamer is separated from her or his true feelings, thus feeling insecure.

Hanging To see a hanged person warns against loneliness and isolation.

Harbour Seeing a harbour indicates that a safe, sheltered place should be sought. There is a need to reorganise and regain confidence before setting sail again over the waters of life.

Hare If the hare in your dreams moves, it means you are following a mystical path, for this animal is associated with legend and myth. On a less poetic level, you can expect to leap ahead towards success.

Harness A harness, whether on a horse or not, indicates hard work ahead.

Harp This musical instrument projects Celtic vibes and has a heavenly influence.

Hat Wearing or seeing a hat in a dream relates to the desire for recognition and respect. A crown is the ultimate hat.

Head Heads symbolise intellect and conscious intentions.

Heart Hearts symbolise intuition and unconscious awareness.

Hearth The centre of the family is represented by a hearth or fireplace. Warmth and affection will be found soon.

Heaven To dream of being in heaven is the dreamer's own version of paradise.

Hedge A restriction, not of the dreamer's own making, surrounds them but it should be fairly easily overcome.

Hell A glimpse of this in a dream warns of a bad time ahead.

Hen A black hen means personal sacrifices will have to be made if you are to reach a goal or achieve an ambition. A white hen means successes will soon be yours.

Herbs Herbs are an urgent reminder telling you to take extra care of your health.

Herd To see a herd of cattle warns you not to be one of many, 'one of the herd'. Be more individualistic.

Hero/Heroine These characters represent the self. They may also represent someone the dreamer admires and unconsciously mimics. Sometimes a celebrity or famous person is used as a model to symbolise this image.

Highway Destiny, the road through life, is symbolised by this.

Hill To climb a hill shows progress is being made towards attaining an aim or goal. To reach the top shows you have or will shortly reach a point in life where you will be able to see ahead clearly. To be going down a hill warns against losing ground in some way.

Hive Hives symbolise communities where many work for the common good.

Hole A hole offers a distinct warning so beware of putting your foot in it.

Holiday Holidays in dreams are signs urging the dreamer to take a break from the routine way of life.

Home To dream of one's home shows the need for protection and comfort within the family.

Honey Honey is the symbol of plenty and future happiness.

Hood A hooded figure is traditionally known as the figure of death.

Horse Horses symbolise power, as in 'horsepower'. In dreams this relates to a person's energy and drive. If you are riding a horse it shows you have control over inner desires.

Horseshoe In myth the horseshoe is associated with the Moon Goddess who rules romance. It is generally a sign of goodwill and good fortune.

Hospital To see a hospital in your dreams can mean you need hospital treatment but on a more symbolic level it indicates the need for hospitality.

Hot To be aware of heat in a dream warns you not to become too close or involved with a certain person or situation.

Hotel Hotels in dreams show a desire to lose one's personal identity and become simply one of a crowd.

House Houses in dreams symbolise the Mansion of the Soul. This is often a composite of all the houses the dreamer has known. The upper part of a house represents the intellect and far-seeing aims; the various rooms relate to different aspects of life, for instance the cellar represents the unconscious recesses of the mind where fears and half-forgotten truths lie hidden.

Hunger To experience this feeling in a dream means that you hunger, and probably thirst, for knowledge, understanding and explanations generally.

Hurricane Destructive forces are in the air when this storm blows up.

Hurt To feel pain in a dream is sometimes the infringement of real pain. Symbolically, the hurt is emotional.

Hymns Hearing hymns in dreams shows you have divine protection so confidence should increase.

I

Ice Total lack of feeling is indicated when ice appears in a dream. Skating on this is a self-explicit, metaphorical warning.

Iceberg Icebergs denote warnings concerning that which lies beneath the surface.

Icon This sacred image may represent the dreamer's worship of someone in particular. Beware of placing this person on a pedestal.

Idol An idol or statue signifies veneration or worship of a person, irrespective of whether they merit it or not.

Illness To feel ill in a dream is usually a health warning and should be taken literally.

Impostor The dream-impostor is usually the dreamer, so be honest with yourself.

Impotence This exclusively male dream-experience warns of the possibility of such a thing. Symbolically, it means the dreamer is powerless or helpless in some way.

Incense Healing and help are represented by the smell of incense.

Injury Receiving physical injury in a dream usually represents an emotional hurt but it should always be considered as a literal warning as well.

Ink An ink blot means that any present trouble has been caused by your own hand. Writing in ink tells you to state your case firmly and clearly.

Inoculation To feel an injection, an inoculation, means you are protected against future emotional trauma.

Insects Insects symbolise small, but nonetheless annoying incidents. Deal with these by brushing them aside.

Intestines See these as a health warning related to digestive problems, but also ask yourself if you have the guts to carry out that special mission, duty or necessary task.

Inventor The inventor in your dream is none other than an aspect of yourself, letting you know that you possess latent talents and originality.

Invisibility Unseen possibilities, as well as unseen problems, may exist.

Iris The iris represents the Goddess Iris who is a messenger of the gods.

Iron This metal symbolises iron will, endurance and strength of purpose. Expect these qualities to be tested.

Island An island represents aloneness which can lead to total self-sufficiency.

Ivy Ivy is a hard-clinging plant so beware of hangers-on.

J

Jade Jade, as a stone or in the form of a statue, means you should not rely on others and their opinions.

Jasmine The scent of jasmine represents healing energy and feminine qualities.

Jay This bird is said to be a messenger from the dead.

Jellyfish Seeing this creature indicates that a mysterious situation or concept exists, that defies logic.

Jerusalem This city, appearing in a dream, symbolises eternal hope.

Jesus Jesus appearing in a dream symbolises God within and God without. He also brings hope, healing and confidence.

Jewellery Beware of self-adornment for the express purpose of attracting attention.

Jewels Jewels and gems represent treasures of the mind; a crystallised plan or brilliant idea will emerge shortly.

Jockey A jockey is that aspect of the dreamer who is well in control of his or her own drive and destiny, even when the going is tough.

Joker This card should not be taken at face value. Do not be deceived by the superficial behaviour of others, for the person to whom this card refers has a very serious side to their nature.

Journey Journeys and movement occur in most dreams — few reflect still life. Whatever the mode of transport — walking, swimming, rising a horse, travelling by bus, etc. — all reflect the way through life; the dreamer's destinational path.

Judge A judge represents the principle 'judge not, that ye be not judged'.

Jug Seeing a jug in your dreams means life holds more than you realise so look forward to much happier times.

Juggler Plans for the future which seem to have gone awry should be rearranged and not abandoned.

Jump To jump from the top of a building or from a cliff metaphorically tells you there are other, safer ways of climbing down, than those you have in mind.

K

Kangaroo This animal represents a restless, elusive person who hops from one thing to another.

Kennel Unless the dreamer is concerned about dogs and their welfare, a kennel warns of the proverbial dog-house.

Kerb Stepping off a kerb in a dream and waking suddenly is known as a myoclonic jerk. This is caused by a muscular contraction which often takes place in early sleep, and has nothing to do with dreams.

Kettle If the kettle in your dream is boiling, beware of situations which may be 'coming to the boil' or on the brink of boiling over.

Key This symbol holds the key to a particular situation so relate its significance to personal circumstances.

Killing To witness the killing of a person or animal means extreme dislike is felt for someone. The figure seen to be killed may, on the other hand, represent a personal trait which the dreamer wishes to eliminate.

King The king is the archetypal father figure; it is also the dominant ruling principle.

Kiss Affection and genuine friendship may be the message of a dream-kiss. It is also a sign of recognition and discrimination.

Kitchen When a dream takes place in a kitchen it shows the theme relates to domestic matters.

Kite To see a flying kite tells the dreamer to be confident and proud of what and who they are.

Kitten Kittens usually represent kittenish characteristics in a person who is normally staid.

Knee When knees are noticed in dreams it is said that the dreamer can expect to meet an important person.

Kneel Kneeling is a humbling sign suggesting more respect is needed for others or someone in particular.

Knife To see a knife warns of quarrels and rows, especially verbal stabs in the back.

Knight The knight is the gallant, chivalrous image of an individual, not necessarily the dreamer.

Knitting Depending on other signs in the dream, knitting represents the pattern of life and whether things are getting into a tangle.

Knocking To hear a knock or knocking is a warning, alerting you in readiness for a surprise or a shock.

Knot Traditionally, a knot symbolises a union or marriage.

L

Labyrinth A mystery or puzzle in life needs to be solved. To do this follow the thread, the causal chain, back to its origin.

Lace This fabric represents a closely guarded or veiled secret.

Ladder A dream-ladder connects two dimensions, heaven and earth, as well as linking consciousness with the unconscious.

Ladybird Although an insect, a ladybird does not signify an annoyance. Instead, it means success, albeit limited, can be anticipated.

Lake Smooth sailing and easier times ahead but remember, still waters run deep.

Lamb A lamp symbolises self-sacrifice.

Land Land or territory represents the environment and surroundings relating to a particular situation.

Lantern If the lantern is hanging up it is to be seen as a warning. If it is resting on a table or shelf, see it as a welcoming sign.

Larder This symbolises emotional reserves which fortify you with food for thought.

Laughter Laughter is always a good sign but remember to laugh only at yourself and not at others.

Lawn Try to cultivate a calm and serene outlook.

Leaf If the leaf is on a tree, life will prosper but if the leaf is on the ground, beware of hardship.

Leather An unfortunate sign of materialistic gain and eventual financial loss.

Lecture Be ready for someone who may try to 'speak down' to you.

Leek Like onions, leeks are signs of good health. They are also the symbol of Wales.

Left/Right To be aware of left and right compares two choices or opposites. Dream scenes are mirror images of reality. This is most noticeable when driving a dream-car — the steering wheel is usually on the wrong side.

Letter Letters symbolise news from afar so expect to hear from someone you have not seen for some time.

Lettuce This vegetable means a pressing problem will be short lived.

Lift See elevator.

Light A light symbolises the light within, the spirit. Metaphorically, it means sudden realisation; having 'seen the light'.

Lighthouse This building is a version of the Mansion of the Soul, where towering ambitions are housed. These will stand up against the roughest of life's storms.

Lily This flower symbolises the Great Mother, the Holy family and French royalty.

Limbs To feel paralysis of the arms and legs is a physical state experienced in early sleep. When incorporated into a dream it seems as if you are rooted to the spot and cannot move. Metaphorically, you could be out on a limb.

Lion Traditionally, a courageous person is represented by a lion in a dream, but beware of testing their strength too far.

Lizard This reptile represents a person who is not as formidable or ugly underneath as they appear on the outside.

Lobster Lobsters reflect shyness — blushing as red as lobster.

Lock Unless there is a key in the lock, this is a warning sign denoting an obstacle.

Looking Glass This provides a reflection of the past and the future.

Lose To lose an object warns of mental tiredness and distractions so take more care over personal matters.

Lost To be lost in an unknown town or country shows feelings of insecurity and lack of plans for the future.

Luggage Luggage, like baggage, is traditionally linked with marriage. It also signifies superficial, personal problems which prevent progress being made.

Lynx This creature represents a quick-witted person.

M

Maggot Expect trouble to creep out of the proverbial woodwork which could bring considerable changes.

Magnet Sex appeal and personal attractiveness are represented by a magnet.

Magpie Traditionally, one magpie is said to be an unlucky sign but if two appear in a dream, good fortune is indicated. Their black and white plumage, in addition, signifies opposites and difficulties in making the right choice.

Man A man appearing in a woman's dream, unless recognised, is usually her animus. If he is feared, he symbolises brute force and masculine traits. In a man's dream, he represents certain characteristics of himself.

Mansion A mansion, a vast house, symbolises the dreamer as a whole — body, mind and spirit.

Manure Generally accepted as a good sign, manure also represents the cycle of life where nothing is wasted or lost.

Map To see a map in a dream reflects your destiny and future plans you have in mind.

Marble Marble, in any shape or form, is a monument to the past.

Marigold This flower is a sign of cheerfulness, happiness in the home and improved social relationships.

Market Markets warn you to select options with care.

Marriage Marriage and weddings represent a union of compatible opposites; they also symbolise the mystical marriage of the soul.

Marsh Marshes warn of unseen dangers so tread carefully.

Martyr When a martyr appears in a dream, distinguish between willing self-sacrifice and grudging martyrdom.

Mask A mask hides the true face of the dreamer so beware of self-deception as well as being deceived by others.

Mass Mass is a healing experience for body and soul.

Mast The mast of a ship in a dream is pointing the way, thus drawing attention to something important yet obvious.

Mat If you walk on a mat in a dream it warns of your being downtrodden; conversely, be careful not to step on others.

Maze A maze symbolises your destiny, showing blind alleys and ways ahead.

Meal Sharing a meal shows a need to communicate and exchange knowledge, information or ideas with others. Eating alone means food for thought is needed.

Meat To eat meat in a dream shows you are assimilating ideas originated by others.

Medicine A health warning may be offered by medicine seen in a dream but if you were taking it, it shows you can 'take your own medicine'.

Medium Mediums in dreams act as messengers from the dead.

Melon This fruit means events will take a turn for the better.

Mermaid Mermaids are water spirits and when they appear in a dream, they are lamenting lost loves.

Meteor A meteor is a warning sign concerning unrest in the future.

Microscope Seeing a microscope in a dream tells you not to see or read too much into a particular situation or it will appear out of all proportion.

Milk Milk is a sign of comfort and human kindness.

Mill Water and windmills indicate a peaceful, prosperous future.

Mirror The truth is reflected in a mirror so you will probably come face to face with yourself.

Mistletoe In addition to its Christmas associations, this plant has parasitic tendencies.

Mole Moles represent spies so beware of those whom you cannot trust.

Money This represents things of value, but not necessarily money in the bank. To receive money tells you that you can expect a reward for deeds done in the past.

Monk A monk symbolises the wise one within.

Monsters These creatures symbolise a monstrous fear and frequently appear in children's dreams. When they chase you it means you are running away from facing a frightening truth.

Moon Femininity and maternal principles are traditionally associated with the moon. Emotions are also affected by this influence so be sure to be in control of these.

Morning This time of day relates to youthfulness and hope so new beginnings are indicated.

Moth Moths symbolise fleeting happiness, especially after dark.

Mother Your mother in your dream usually symbolises feminine principles and maternal feelings of compassion.

Motor Cycle This vehicle tells you that life will speed up considerably soon.

Mountain Depending on the circumstances in the dream, a mountain represents either an obstacle which seems immovable, or a pinnacle in life which should be attained.

Mouse This little creature represents timidity; it also tells you to lie low and keep quiet until danger has passed.

Moving Moving house, when you don't intend to, tells you to change your image.

Mud Expect mixed blessings from a situation which at present seems to be causing worry and frustration.

Museum This building is a repository of past glories and antiquated ideas, so its message is 'live for today, not yesterday'.

Mushrooms Mushrooms have mystical connotations.

Music To hear music symbolises life with its harmonies and discords, its high and low notes. Metaphorically, maybe you have to face the music, or on the other hand, perhaps someone is playing on your emotions.

N

Nail To see nails warns of dangers, especially from external sources.

Naked To be without clothes in a dream shows the real self; personality, habits or secrets are bared for the world to see. All pretence is dropped and the truth is or will be revealed.

Names A name is usually a reminder concerning someone you should contact. Certain names may not mean anything to you at the time of the dream but later prove to have been prophetic.

Narrow A narrow path or corridor indicates certain limitations, showing there is no choice but to go on.

Neck This part of the anatomy means you should not take chances or risk losing everything.

Needle Beware of those who try to 'needle' you and at the same time try to make amends.

Neighbour Your neighbour in your dream is none other than yourself.

Nest A nest symbolises the home.

Net A net is an obvious trap so walk carefully.

New Year Traditionally this time of year tells you to begin again with renewed hope.

Niece Youthful femininity and loyal family support are represented by a niece.

Night To be aware that a dream takes place during the night shows you are 'in the dark', so you should try to throw light on a perplexing situation.

Nightmare This is a bad dream based on a fear arising from many different sources. Its origin is that of the legendary mare who ran wild and devoured her own sons.

North Darkness, winter and the colder things in life are symbolised by this direction, including death.

Numbers The dreaming mind is a calendar so dates, anniversaries and appointments are often indicated as numbers. Specific numbers sometimes relate to a definite number of hours, days or years, as in the Pharaoh's dream of the seven kine and ears of corn.

Nun A nun symbolises the wise woman within as well as an especially revered person.

Nymph This is a dream messenger.

O

Oak This tree represents steadfastness within the family as well as the proverbial 'hearts of oak' mentality. It also has Druidic associations.

Oar Direction and effort should be put into your life.

Oats Traditionally oats relate to sexual appetite.

Observatory This building houses long-sighted vision so look beyond the horizon.

Ocean Vast emotional potential is reflected by the turbulent or calm state of your dream ocean.

Office Unless an office in a dream is to be taken literally, it symbolises the filing system in the Mansion of the Soul — the memory.

Ogre An ogre is usually the archetype representing the threatening father.

Oil To see oil tells you to act as the peacemaker, so metaphorically pour it over troubled waters.

Ointment This symbolises healing and healing remedies, especially those in the form of a balm.

Old Man He is the wise old man within, who has learned much from past experiences.

Old Woman She is the wise old woman within, who has learned much from past experiences.

Olives Peace and a connection with the Holy Land are suggested by olives.

Opal This stone warns of certain circumstances which could become disturbing.

Operation Surgical operations in dreams mean you should beware of a calculated invasion of your personal rights.

Opium When this appears in your dream beware of those who would dupe you into submission.

Orchard In dreams an orchard represents part of the proverbial Garden of Eden, offering a reward reaped from the harvest of life.

Orchestra Be sure to keep in tune and in harmony with others.

Orchid This flower is always associated with passionate love.

Ornaments To see these in a dream warns you of false standards.

Ostrich High-flying aims will not get off the ground easily, but do not bury your head in the sand.

Owl In Greek tradition the owl symbolised the Mother Goddess and Athene. It is, today, still a sign of wisdom.

Oxen Mundane tasks and heavy burdens will or are being carried.

Oxygen Inspiration and a new awakening can be expected when oxygen appears in a dream.

Oyster This shellfish symbolises the world, which could be yours for the taking.

P

Pain To feel pain in a dream can be a warning sign concerning physical health but it may also relate to an emotional wound.

Parachute A parachute offers a possible way out of a difficult situation.

Paralysed The feeling of paralysis in sleep is not a dream but an awareness of physical immobility which occurs naturally during the early stages of sleep. When this paralysis is incorporated into a dream it seems as if you are rooted to the spot.

Parcel To see a parcel means you can expect a happy surprise.

Parents Inherited attributes as well as inferior qualities are reflected in dream parents, in the hope that they may be recognised in oneself.

Parrot Beware of repeated, worthless chatter.

Parsley This herb has traditional links with the feminine principles of healing and homemaking, hence the superstition that only the wife who is dominant in a relationship can grow it.

Party A party in a dream reflects social activities and the making of new friends.

Pattern Patterns symbolise 'life's rich pattern' which is formed from various experiences.

Peach This fruit symbolises bitter-sweet memories.

Peacock Peacocks symbolise male dominance and are a sign warning against boasting.

Pearls These are tears of the Moon Goddess and it is for this reason that they are regarded as unlucky.

Peas When peas appear in a dream they tell you of difficulties in making the right choice.

Pen Since the pen is said to be mightier than the sword, this object warns of libellous writing.

Penguin Birds that cannot fly, such as penguins, reflect limitations imposed on high-flying aims and ambitions.

Photograph A photograph of an individual is a reminder concerning the subject of someone of whom they remind you.

Picture The scene depicted represents a situation which can be seen literally or abstractly.

Pig This creature depicts a person the dreamer dislikes.

Pigeon Town and country influences will affect plans when this bird appears in a dream.

Pillars Pillars offer strong support, thus offer confidence too.

Plants Plants symbolise life, therefore the nature and state of those seen in a dream are important.

Plastic When plastic is obvious in a dream, beware of artificial or false feelings.

Play A play relates to an episode in the dreamer's life.

Plough All the effort that has been put into ploughing ahead in life, especially when the going is hard, is reflected by this object.

Plums Ideal conditions are indicated when plums appear in a dream.

Police Authority, law and order are signified by this force. Depending on circumstances in the dream, this may relate to orderliness within the dreamer or to external events.

Pond A pool of emotion is signified by this water.

Potatoes These represent human responses to the basic problems of a so-called earthy nature.

Prayer Prayers in dreams symbolise a call for help and guidance.

Pregnant To be pregnant or see someone who is pregnant in a dream, means ideas have been conceived which have great potential in the future.

Primrose Romantic relationships, like this flower, need very careful handling.

Prison Life can seem like a prison so beware of self-made restrictions.

Puppet A warning that someone is pulling your strings, manipulating you, is indicated when a puppet appears in a dream.

Pyramid Ancient Egypt is symbolised by a pyramid but from a more personal point of view it tells you that to reach the point you are aiming for, you should start from a broad base and work your way up slowly.

Python This snake is a dream messenger for it traditionally symbolises Pythea, the Greek oracular priestess.

Q

Quarry Make every effort to discover the truth for, as the saying goes, 'the answer lies in a stone'.

Quartet The four-fold nature of life and the four elements of creation are represented by a harmonious quartet.

Quay Make the most of the present calm before a storm blows up.

Queen To dream of a queen represents feelings of equality and familiarity. She also symbolises the feminine principles embodied by Mother Nature as well as the queen found in storybook romances.

Quicksand The undoubted warning quicksand offers is that of being swallowed up by some awful situation.

Quoits As a game, quoits represents the skilful game of loving, in the Freudian sense, and living, from the standpoint of chance.

R

Rabbi To see a rabbi in a dream introduces a Judaic influence and thoughts concerning the Old Testament.

Rabbits Fertility and breeding instincts are suggested by rabbits. A white rabbit, as in Alice in Wonderland, leads the dreamer into his or her own inner world.

Race This activity indicates that the pace of life is increasing unnecessarily. Rivalry between the dreamer and others should be considered.

Radio Telepathic messages, external influences and communication are indicated when radios appear in your dream.

Raft To be on a raft shows you have been rescued from a dangerous situation but beware of drifting into further trouble.

Rags Rags tell the dreamer that poor circumstances can be improved (rags to riches), but personal effort has to be exerted to attain this.

Railway Station Destiny and which line to take in life is under consideration when you seem to be at a station in your dream, so make plans for the future which will keep you on the right lines.

Rain Seeing rain in a dream is a good sign telling you that troubles will be washed away eventually.

Rainbow Hopes will rise and the proverbial pot of gold at the end of the rainbow awaits you.

Ram Masculine over-dominance is suggested when this animal appears in a dream. He may also represent a person born under the sign of Aries.

Rape Apart from the obvious warning which should be taken literally, try to avoid those who force you to do something against your will or better judgement.

Raven A raven or crow symbolises the Celtic spirit of Bran and Britain, hence the ravens in residence at the Tower of London.

Recipe A recipe is a prescription for better health.

Religious Experiences These experiences show that spiritual beliefs need to be expressed, possibly in a practical way.

Reservoir An accumulation of water represents a storehouse of emotional energy.

Restaurant A dream set in a restaurant shows that the dreamer is in need of food for thought — sustenance for body, mind and spirit.

Rhinoceros Traditionally this creature is seen as a symbol of sex and fertility.

Rice Good news is to be expected on the home front. Weddings, not surprisingly, may also be expected.

Riding Riding a horse or any other animal means mastery and conquest of a person, talent, energy, drive or even a handicap.

Right See left/right.

Ring A ring represents a long, unbroken friendship as anticipated by the giving of engagement and wedding rings.

River Seeing a river in a dream warns that your life may be flowing by too swiftly.

Road The dream road is your way through life, your destinational highway along which are encountered hazards and happiness.

Robber A robber in your dream warns of loss of face, identity or credibility.

Robin This bird is traditionally recognised as a messenger from the dead.

Rocks These usually warn of 'being on the rocks', so beware of impending dangers.

Room A room represents an aspect of the dreamer. The kitchen denotes domestic matters, the bedroom close relationships, the attic ideals and the basement is where fears and half-forgotten memories reside.

Roots Stability, confidence and strength of purpose are symbolised by roots.

Rope A strong attachment to a person or place is indicated.

Roses These flowers signify a message of deep feeling — depending on their colour.

Rooted to the Spot See paralysis.

Running You may be running towards a goal, or running away from something or someone you cannot face.

S

Sack Seeing a sack in a dream tells you that something, possibly the future, holds more than is apparent at present.

Sacrifice A sacrifice of any living thing in a dream tells you that you must not be afraid of sacrificing some of your own interests for the good of others.

Saddle To be in the saddle is a sign telling you that you are in a controlling position but you must know where you are going or all will be wasted.

Sage This herb is associated with physical healing.

Sailing Sailing on smooth water tells you things will improve but if there is a strong wind blowing or the water is rough, take this as a warning sign.

Saint A saint represents someone who can be relied upon, whatever the circumstances.

Salad Thoughts of a philosophical nature are represented by live food of this nature.

Sale To be at a sale means you can expect bargains in life.

Salmon This fish was sacred to the early Britons so seek out Celtic links and ancestry.

Salt This mineral is said to be the essence of life.

Sand Dry sand represents annoyances which are trivial and not lasting, but wet sand warns of old ideas which cling to the present.

Sapphire This stone, along with all gems, reflects aspects of the inner self, the soul.

Satellite Watch out for those on the periphery who could take over your life or a situation which is at present under your control.

Saw A saw, whether using it or not, indicates a cutting down to size.

Scar Scars shows that an emotional wound from the past is healed, but is not forgotten.

Scent An influence manifesting through the sense of smell. This is usually associated with certain aromas which, in dreams, bring back past memories.

School Schools symbolise life which is made up of various lessons from which we are supposed to learn and thus evolve.

Scientists The head, the intellect, rules when scientists intrude into a dream; intuition and the heart need to be expressed more.

Scissors Any unnecessary links or ties should be cut.

Sea See ocean.

Seeds Great potential for the future is offered when seeds appear in a dream, provided they are sown at the right time.

Serpent A serpent, especially when it twists and turns, symbolises emotional energy and an entanglement which is difficult to throw off.

Sewing Sewing represents industriousness.

Sex From the Freudian point of view, sex in a dream is a submerged urge but symbolically it may represent guilty feelings in no way associated with sex.

Shadow The shadows seen in dreams is the neglected side of the dreamer although it may also reflect a fear cast by someone else.

Shapes Shapes, especially geometric, form the basis of the language of the mind. They also represent life when it conforms too much to a strict pattern.

Sheep To see sheep in a dream tells you to be individualistic and not to be easily led.

Ship To be on a ship in a dream represents life's voyage over troubled waters, as well as smooth crossings.

Shoes Seeing shoes in a dream tells you to follow in someone else's footsteps. Conversely, the dream may be telling you to see someone else's point of view as if you were in their shoes.

Shops Shops tell you there are several choices so do not make up your mind too hastily.

Silk This fabric suggests luxury and an easy or easier life in the future.

Silver This metal is associated with the mind and flashes of illumination.

Singing Singing is a good sign to hear in a dream telling you that help will come from a superior level.

Sister This woman in a dream represents feminine support generally but if there is disagreement with a sister, it means lack of harmony exists within the dreamer.

Skeleton The proverbial skeleton in the cupboard is represented by this.

Sky The sky is the limit so be confident and go for that aim or goal.

Sledge Like other vehicles, sledges show how the dreamer is progressing along his or her personal highway of life.

Sleep To sleep in a dream tells you that its message is being reinforced, doubly.

Slide To slide or to see a slide warns of losing control.

Smoke Slow, twisting smoke warns of death.

Snakes These reptiles represent human energies in their various forms, from sexual demands to ruthless, ambitious drive. They also symbolise the healing arts.

Snow Emotional coldness, bleakness and lack of warmth generally are indicated by snow in a dream.

Soldier A soldier may symbolise the dreamer's brave hero. On the other hand, the military discipline this image conjures up suggests life should be more orderly.

South Sunnier, warmer climes or times are forecast by this direction.

Sparrow A chirpy person, possibly a cockney, is signified by a sparrow.

Spider The dream spider may represent the feminine devouring affection of woman. If it is a small spider, it could be a money-spinner but whichever it is, always beware of entanglements and traps — the web.

Spirit A spirit is either a memory from the past or the ghost of a person.

Square This shape symbolises a situation on an 'all square basis', showing a well-regulated, stable lifestyle.

Stag A bachelor is represented by a stag.

Stairs Going upstairs indicates a rise in status, promotion, success and acclaim. Going downstairs shows loss of recognition and confidence.

Star A star symbolises your destiny. It may also herald the birth of a baby.

Statue This image is probably someone whom the dreamer has put on a pedestal and idolises.

Stones Stones convey cold-heartedness and lack of compassion, not to mention hard feelings.

Sun The sun is the supreme symbol offering hope, brilliance and happiness.

Swan This bird is a sign of the White Goddess, the mother of creation.

Swimming Effort put into life at the emotional level is symbolised by swimming in your dream.

Sword A sword is a sign of defence as well as attack.

T

Table Tables represent altars upon which the dreamer places beliefs, thoughts and hopes. Self-sacrifice is also indicated by this object.

Tap To hear a tap or rap means someone wishes to contact you or draw your attention to something important.

Tarantula This warns you that you are probably your own worst enemy.

Taxi Take advantage of help offered to you by others but know that in the end it is that which you do for yourself that is the most valuable.

Tea An innocent friendship is represented by drinking or serving tea to others.

Teacher A teacher is an aspect of the dreamer — the wise self within.

Tears Tears symbolise emotional relief but sometimes they are associated with an inner sadness.

Teeth Changes in the pattern and the pace of life, such as leaving school and starting work, changing jobs, moving, getting married or divorced, etc., are symbolised by either loose teeth or teeth which are falling out.

Telephone Telephones represent communication, such as getting in touch with your inner self, or contacting another.

Temple This building represents a private place within yourself; it is the place you retire to, to reflect upon the outer world.

Thread A thread, sometimes golden, symbolises the link between body and soul, heaven and earth.

Theatre This is the theatre of the mind where images act out thoughts.

Thunder The sound of thunder represents a powerful warning from an authoritative source.

Tide Tides symbolise ebbing and flowing emotions.

Tiger A sign of physical energy, drive and enthusiasm.

Time Hours, days, weeks, months or years signify the passing of time. The number associated with these indicates the time involved.

Toilet Lavatories represent the basic needs in life, especially the more personal ones. They also signify the elimination of unwanted memories which should be flushed away.

Tomb A tomb warns against restrictions which surround the dreamer, indicating these should be broken down as soon as possible.

Tower Towering ambitions which tend to isolate the dreamer in a solitary world are symbolised by a tower.

Train Travelling on a train symbolises the dreamer's journey or destiny through life. 'Keeping on the right lines' is important.

Treasure Priceless, unique ideas and precious memories are represented by treasure in a dream.

Trees Family matters are symbolised by trees, ranging from family problems within the family tree, to remote branches and ancestral roots.

Triangle Stability and protection are symbolised by this figure.

Tunnel Tunnels symbolise the connection between this world and the next, and between the conscious and unconscious aspects of mind.

Twins The dual aspects or both sides of a problem or situation are represented by twins.

U

UFO To see this object means you are searching for and finding your own inner light and illumination — your soul.

Umbrella Seeing this in a dream means the dreamer should look for shelter from life's downpours and storms.

Uncle This relative symbolises a reliable, masculine friend who will help in time of need.

Undertaker To see an undertaker in your dream means you have a very unpleasant task to 'undertake'.

Undressed Being undressed in a dream means personal secrets may be revealed unless due care is taken to cover them up properly.

Unicorn This mythological creature symbolises purity, virginity and compassionate beliefs.

Uniform Seeing those in uniform in a dream shows the dreamer has an eye for conformity as well as respect for authority.

University A university represents ancient seats and centres of learning inherent in the dreamer.

Urine Urine in dreams often symbolises relief or the need to let go of those things that really do not matter.

V

Vaccination To be vaccinated in your dream tells you that you are protected, that is immune, from emotional and verbal attacks.

Valley A valley shows life is restricted at present and the future is difficult to see.

Vegetables Life and energy are symbolised by vegetables so note the freshness of any seen in a dream.

Veil The truth is being hidden from the dreamer.

Velvet This fabric warns of what may lie beneath the surface, so do not be lured into false security.

Vest If the vest is too short it shows a lack of confidence and a fear of exposure.

Village A village shows that good foundations exist but these are only the beginning of something greater.

Vinegar Do not be deceived. Vinegar represents problems which are not as bad as they seem.

Voice The voice in a dream is the small, quiet voice within, even when it shouts or is incoherent.

Violets Violets symbolise the spirit.

Violin Emotional harmony can confidently be expected, but expect some pulling at the proverbial heart strings.

Volcano An explosive situation is to be expected so try to recognise signs leading to this.

Vomit To see vomit means you can expect an unpleasant situation — one of which you are sick — soon to be resolved.

Voyage A voyage traditionally means travelling abroad; it also symbolises life's journey over troubled and calmer waters.

Vulture Beware of a vicious competitor waiting to move in and take his or her pick.

W

Waiter To be a waiter in a dream shows your role to be one of service to others.

Walking Walking symbolises the dreamer making his or her way through life.

Wall Walls are obstacles which should be got over, round or overcome.

Wallet The wallet is the masculine equivalent of the feminine handbag. It is that aspect of the dreamer which holds personal beliefs, ideals and private thoughts. To lose it means loss of self-esteem and confidence.

Wallflower This flower represents the odd one out.

Walnuts These nuts assure that the dreamer will be well provided for, although luxuries will be few.

War Conflict of this nature shows the dreamer is against something or someone, or even an aspect of him- or herself.

Washing To wash or be washed symbolises the washing away of problems and negativity from the past.

Wasp To be stung by a wasp warns that enemies are close at hand.

Watch A watch alerts you to the fact that time is marching on.

Water Water symbolises the unconscious self. Heartfelt emotions and feelings which run deep are expressed through this element. It also represents the spiritual waters of life.

Wealth Wealth in a dream does not usually refer to money in the bank. Symbolically it shows the dreamer has a wealth of friends, understanding and wisdom.

Weaving The pattern of life's rich pattern, woven in time through experience, is seen in a dream as the weaving of cloth.

Web A spider's web in a dream warns of an unseen trap from which escape is virtually impossible.

Wedding See marriage.

Well Depth of feeling is symbolised by a well.

West To be aware of this point of the compass in a dream tells the dreamer which direction, albeit metaphorically, to take.

Whale The feminine aspect of the self as well as the womb of Mother Nature is symbolised by a whale.

Wheat Fertility, rebirth and plenty are symbolised by wheat in a dream.

Wheel Traditionally, a wheel represents cycles of life: depending on circumstances it may warn you not to go in circles.

Whistle To hear a whistle in your dream is a warning sign.

Willow Family problems and temporary sadness are indicated by this tree.

Wind Winds of change are signified by a breeze felt in a dream.

Winter This season symbolises a quiet, resting time.

Witch To see a witch warns of disenchantment with someone, or with oneself.

Wolf A wolf warns of hard times ahead.

Woods Families and communities are symbolised by woods.

Wool Wool in a dream reassures the dreamer of protection from verbal blows.

Worm A worm represents terrestrial energies.

X

X-ray Unseen, energetic changes are at work which will bring considerable changes.

Xylophone When this musical instrument appears in a dream it means you should try to keep in tune with others and life generally.

Y

Yawning When you yawn in a dream it tells you that you need to escape from a boring situation.

Yeast Yeast appearing in a dream means that nature will take its course.

Yew This tree represents family problems which cannot be altered.

Z

Zebra This animal represents choice and chance.

Zodiac Seeing the zodiac in a dream means fame and fortune are in the balance.

Zoo A zoo in your dream represents the world, populated by the many different members of the human race.